A Sense of Life, A Sense of Sin

A Sense of Life,
A Sense of Sin

Eugene Kennedy

DOUBLEDAY & COMPANY, INC.

GARDEN CITY, NEW YORK

1975

Excerpt from *Long Day's Journey into Night* by Eugene O'Neill reprinted by permission of Yale University Press. Copyright © 1955 by Carlotta Monterey O'Neill.

Excerpt from *The Flies* by Jean-Paul Sartre, from *No Exit and The Flies*, trans. by Stuart Gilbert. Copyright © 1946 by Stuart Gilbert. Reprinted by permission of Alfred A. Knopf, Inc.

Library of Congress Cataloging in Publication Data

Kennedy, Eugene
  A sense of life, a sense of sin.

  1. Ethics. 2. Sin. I. Title.
BJ1012.K43   241
ISBN 0-385-09538-4
Library of Congress Catalog Card Number 74-25110

Copyright © 1975 by Eugene Kennedy
All Rights Reserved
Printed in the United States of America
First Edition

CONTENTS

	Introduction	9
1	The Catholic Conflict	13
2	The End of Romantic America	27
3	A Sense of Life	38
4	A Sense of Sin	50
5	A Sense of Values	60
6	A Sense of Ourselves	70
7	A Sense of Responsibility	80
8	Living	93
9	Sinning	104
10	Can Anyone Sin Anymore?	116
11	Some Real Sins	124
12	A Sense of Passion	141
13	A Sense of the Spirit	154
14	A Sense of Wholeness	164
15	Common Sense	179

A Sense of Life, A Sense of Sin

INTRODUCTION

This book is not about moral theology but about moral living. Granted that there should be no distinction between these topics, it remains true that the technical apparatus of moral theology, like that of advanced statistics, is not easily translatable into the everyday language of life. Advanced statistics can, of course, describe the human condition with all that you gain in efficiency and all that you lose in a feel for living by using numbers. The problem is not as intense but it is quite similar for moral theology, which cannot abandon its tradition, its constructs, nor its slow-paced discipline in exploring moral principles. The same risk of losing a feel for everyday living is present; it is, in fact, echoed in the remark of the average person after a perusal of complicated moral principles, "Yes, but is it right or wrong for me to do this?"

This work is connected with the struggle most persons experience in applying moral principles in the course of their lives and work. Does sin exist anymore? The question is neither irrelevant nor uncommon these days. It is a signal of the individual challenge to shape and sustain a moral position in a bewildering world. Our moral presence in life has always depended on how seriously we take this invitation to responsibility for our own moral decisions.

We are only now becoming aware of how difficult it is to
lead an adult moral life. This is not because the temptations
are so overwhelming but because life is never trifling. What
we do, how we feel, how we react to each other: All these
things make a difference because out of the mass of our
human activities we establish our permanent and defining
moral presence. Morality is connected with actions, yes, but
our actions are connected always with our persons, and it is
only as we come to grips with our total selves that we write
our authentic moral signature on life. Morality does not
consist in following the right directions, no matter how sensitively these may be described by those outside of us, but
in making our own informed way through the unique terrain of our lives.

The simplest thesis of this book can only be stated inadequately. In order to be moral we have to take our existence seriously, something that extremes of spirituality and
materialism make difficult for us. Some forms of religion
have made it hard for persons to take their lives seriously
because they have underplayed the value of this world; extreme hedonism does the same thing through distorting our
image of personality in just the opposite direction. If you
emphasize denial, you estrange people from ever experiencing their wholeness as human beings; if you emphasize sensual pleasure excessively, you do the same thing. The moral
struggle is involved in seeing ourselves whole and in taking
seriously the meaning of our one-time-only experience of
life in the human situation. We are not supposed to huddle
in fear at the edge of the universe waiting until life merci-
fully ends; neither are we to exploit or mindlessly destroy
ourselves in a single-minded and selfish quest for a sensual
nirvana. Life is the medium through which we express and
experience our meaning. Taking ourselves seriously is a necessary precondition for this.

Taking ourselves seriously does not mean that we should

take ourselves solemnly. Part of our redemption lies in laughter, in the forgiving and reviving showers of mirth that cleanse and renew us. Being serious about life does, however, mean that we take our individual, imperfect selves with appropriate respect for our possibilities and opportunities in the life we share together. That involves us in developing our capacities and talents as persons and of finely honing our sensitivity to the way we influence each other all the time. There is a vague contemporary dream about a neutral moral place where we can do anything we please because no one else knows and no one else will be hurt. Lots of what is best in life is invisible, and that barren spot where we think that we are safe from moral inspection and moral consequences simply does not exist. When we take our existence with sufficient seriousness, we know that we always make some difference, if only to ourselves, in the way we make ourselves present in life.

Forming our consciences, regarding each other and the needs of our communities with operational respect, confessing and celebrating our involvement in the human enterprise: These are the common actions through which we reveal our moral stature and our personal meaning. This book is written to spur and help people reflect on the good and evil that is within their power to effect. This is not a how-to-do-it book but an invitation and encouragement to live more deeply, more responsibly, and more compassionately. The most important part of taking our moral lives seriously lies in taking our experience of incarnation seriously too. The moral and religious lives go together, and those who understand this are the discoverers of both joy and meaning.

Eugene Kennedy
F.S.

1

The Catholic Conflict

Being a Catholic does indeed make a difference in a person's life. What are the themes which, while not the exclusive property of the Catholic tradition, have been accented in a particular way by it? The first of these centers on the world view which, up until very recent years, was maintained with extraordinary integrity throughout Catholic cultures and subcultures. The eyes of faith allowed the Catholic to structure the universe in a unique and consistent fashion. Through them Catholics could look beyond this world and the evidence of ourselves to the intensely real supernatural sphere, to the heaven that ransomed the suffering and death of everyday existence, to the salvation mediated by the Church and its sacramental life and merited by a dutiful Christian existence.

The motivating power of this firmly held vision of a hierarchially ordered universe has been enormous both in enabling Catholics to handle their experience of suffering and in releasing the energies for educational, parochial, and missionary enterprises. This view was sustained by enormous resources of symbolism, which, in a cumulative way, built an extraordinary sense of the eternal dimension of life. The pool of symbols—from holy water to ashes to the miracles at Lourdes, from the vaulted spaces of great churches to the ingrained rhythms of plainchant—was large and deep enough to cleanse anyone of the grime of this world. The transcendent was underscored in a thousand ways, and this generated an amazing spiritual self-confidence about heavenly rewards as well as an undervaluing of this world, earthly crowns, and even scientific achievement. The Church stood against the world, which was coupled with the flesh and the devil, pointing always beyond to the only true home for the yearning pilgrim. Home lay across the horizon, and one did not properly tarry nor grow attached to the things or scenes of this world. The sufferings of this time were not to be counted against the glory to come. Such powerful visions lead to mixed consequences; everyone who has grown up in a Catholic culture has felt them.

If, for example, one characteristic Catholic attitude was to despise this world, then the self and one's talents—even the possibilities of one's achievements—could be thrown willingly onto the sacrificial fire. Overcoming the self meant achieving a mastery of the body and an exaltation of the spirit; the Catholic sense of values proposed an absolute and a heroic journey toward it. The negative implications of despising the body, ignoring the world's more urgent problems, and living with bags packed for the imminent parousia have been articulated clearly during the last decade. Was this, however, all loss, a viewpoint only to be regretted? Or was there something here that shaped the Catholic soul in a way not to be despised? Part of the extraordinary mystery of living in the environment of the Catholic Church lay not only in the strongly reinforced sense of identity that it delivered but also in the special sense of presence in and through time that it offered. Living as a Catholic altered a person's sense of time, breaking its binds not only in the action of the Eucharist but through collapsing the centuries of history so that one could feel a kinship with fellow Catholics across the ages. The Catholics would only come late to a feeling of being orphans of modern times because they were so at home with the Christian persons and places—with the saints and shrines—of twenty light and dark centuries. The whole stance of believing Catholics relieved them of the oppression of time; they lived in their own time and place but were never out of relationship to a family of saints and sinners whose timeless presence stood behind the statues and medals, and in the holy persons who could be prayed to for every need beyond the flickering banks of votive candles. There were, in other words, practical ways of not just remembering a glorious past but of constantly re-experiencing it, of inhabiting the spacious myth of Christendom in the living presence of the community of the saints. Seeing around the curve of time enabled Catholics always to see more than what seemed to be contained in physical reality. Miracles could be believed, a sense of the numinous quivered at the edge of every day; there was indeed more to be sensed about our destiny than just the facts. This contributed in no small measure to the sacramental consciousness of the universe that was a distinctive aspect of traditional Catholic experience.

Of paramount importance in the Catholic awareness was the experience of authority; there is little doubt that this was imprinted in the believer's soul from the earliest age and that even Catholics who feel that they have said good-bye to all that still sense its traces in their souls. The Church operated in a frankly authoritarian manner and, in a huge effort to hold itself together against the challenges of history, it imposed elaborate and effective controls on the lives of its subjects. The inheritance of this emphasis was a conditioned readiness to respect and accede to authority of all kinds—civil and ecclesiastical—and while it made good citizens, good soldiers, and generations of good policemen, it did so at an enormous psychological price. One hardly needs to review the emphasis on conformity that was writ in such bold letters on Catholic life. It was an extraordinary blend of conditioning techniques, not less effective for having been unconsciously adopted. As B. F. Skinner admits, the Church built Walden Two long before he offered his design for it. Proper behavior—the desired response for the virtuous life—was positively reinforced in a thousand symbolic ways. Indeed, the whole chain of behavior that was explicitly stated in the rules of various forms of religious life was sustained by the distant but powerfully reinforcing reward of heaven's promise. Add the principles of aversive conditioning from another branch of psychological behaviorism, and even the thought of evil was so punishing that it would be immediately rejected. No one even had to be looking; you supervised yourself.

Mixed in with this was a steady demand for freely accepted responsibility, for listening to the voice of conscience in the face of all other persuasions, of being a free person who spoke his own *yes* to the Catholic creed. The experience of being accountable in the sight of God for all one's thoughts and actions—the sense of living in a Divine Judge's presence and of having no place to hide—constituted powerful, almost unforgettable parameters of Catholic experience. The Church constructed a portable environment so that Catholics carried their religion deep within them and could never quite run or fall far enough away from it. Even those who have broken away from the institutional Church never seem fully able to escape their religious experience, even if it looms only as something against which they can more clearly define themselves. Something so strong and challenging, even when judged absurd, was not to be shrugged off easily; they have lingering respect—and sometimes affection —for their adversary. Even a brief look at the long lines of exiled Catholic artists and writers bears a mysterious witness to this truth. The tight boundaries of the institutional Church seemed to make it uncomfortable for many searching and creative individuals. The story is familiar: The artist confronts and rejects the tradition of the official Church ("He lost his faith," the abiding believers are told). It seems a condition of creativity for many. The list is long just in America: Dreiser, Hemingway, Fitzgerald, O'Hara, O'Neill, Farrell . . . Jimmy Breslin, referring to the Catholic Church as the "Marine Corps of all churches," says that a man cannot write unless he rebels against it. But Catholicism does not depart from the lives or works of these men; they may break from the Catholic tradition, but they are not outside it. The Church is a presence in their writings, a force, a power that can be felt even when it is criticized or rejected.

If one consults the works of Catholic artists and poets who have remained in the Church, the great themes of sin and salvation, of the mystery of good and evil, sin and forgiveness, of the never quite stifled pressures of conscience, are quite evident. There is always the commanding challenge of the mediating Church, the beckoning of the absolute, the mystique of the rock plunged into eternity. A portion of the lasting fascination of the Church—of the lingering hold it has on the imagination of many of those who have lived in or with it—was its very vastness and seeming imperturbability. Something, one thinks, like Everest, something *there* that had to be taken on its own terms, outlasting the weather of history and the endless forays of climbers trying for a brief moment to conquer it. The imagery of an unchanging presence in human affairs has both attracted and disturbed people, breaking the hold of time and yet, in its secure self-containment, seeming immune to progress as well. The security of the symbol looked inviting to those looking for a place to stand against the shifting winds of time, while its craggy unresponsiveness to change repelled many others.

Something of this mythic changeless quality seemed to play a role in the conversion or return to the Church that could be observed in the lives of certain writers and poets. One thinks of the English writers of the past several generations and of the almost solemn return to tradition that membership in the Roman Catholic Church meant to them. Exercises in psychohistory may only be speculative at best, but two qualities seem to have touched generations of Englishmen from Newman through Knox, Greene, Waugh, down now even to the erratic film maker Ken Russell, who describes himself as a "sinning Catholic." The first is the staying power of the Church, the beyond-time quality of its teeming mythic presence in the middle of history. The second was the absolute demand quality of this Church, the uncompromising insistence that you give up everything, in a sense, that you submit in order to live in it. There is a powerful mystique to such an invitation; it was just such a beckoning that so many artists seemed to hear shortly after the Second World War. Thus becoming a Catholic had a certain fashionableness to it that seemed to reinforce the artist's own commitment. Thus poet Alan Tate and the searching Thomas Merton in our own country. The grail could be found no matter how difficult the journey; the unchanging Jesus lived in and through the fabled Church. Not the least of what the Church offered was the power to handle guilt, the power to forgive sin.

One hardly needs to describe the kind of guilt that has been associated with the Catholic experience. It is by no means only a neurotic difficulty, however, and we are far from understanding the complexity of the situation. That certain aspects of the institution generated guilt is undeniable; that the institution also stood as a forum in which persons could confront and deal with their experiences of guilt is also true. I speak now from a psychological point of view almost exclusively in wonder at the genius of auricular confession, for example, which allowed people to verbalize their sins, to accuse themselves out loud so that they could hear the charges that they brought against themselves and to have them acknowledged and ritually forgiven by God's representative. The therapeutic value of such a response on an individual level—the fact that sin could be dealt with explicitly in relationship to God—would be hard to overestimate. It matched the needs of human nature and, despite the development of communal penance rites, it still does. The Church has the power to deal with sin and guilt, one of the perennial existential problems that is manifested in a strange contemporary way by the urge to confess publicly that can be seen on television talk shows.

One must also acknowledge that the power to deal with sin, like any great power, can be abused. The generalization of inappropriate guilt to a wide range of human actions was one of the effects of this in the Catholic experience. Guilt spread like a stain across the lives of many Catholics who had been overindoctrinated with a sense of their potential sinfulness. If God knew our hearts and there was no hiding from him, then one could only mournfully confront the inevitable accumulation of shortcomings that occurred every day. The human condition was a vulnerable place for those charged with being perfect. Thus the classic Catholic conflict developed: the obsessive effort to be good and to please the all-seeing Divinity and to keep clear of sin. The obsessive approach to living is not, of course, found only among Catholics. We cannot, however, only blame the Puritan ethic for the driven quality of many Catholic lives. The obsessive urge to please may be one of the major characteristics of those Catholics who were caught up in the operational distortion of the Church's teachings on sin. The consequences of failing to be perfect were enormous; the need to find the right way—the exact route through the minefield of life—in order to feel approved here and hereafter became a strong dynamic in Catholic life. It moved persons to forsake their own freedom in order to discover the code or rule from outside themselves that would guarantee that they were doing the right thing and thereby deliver a sense of security. For many Catholics freedom, as Camus once wrote, was "too heavy to bear."

The Church—the perfect society of laws—would tell us what to do in order to be saved. One can only marvel at the sincerity and earnestness of so many Catholics who broke themselves on the slowly turning wheel of obsessive perfectionism. This tendency to offer a detailed account of the good life was in many ways a departure from and a betrayal of the more mystical and symbolic aspects of the Church's life. One is tempted to say that the Church, like a poet, is at its best when it does not quite know what it is doing and when it does not self-consciously try to analyze the process by which it is present to persons. Excessive intellectualization destroys mythical symbolization; trying to explain everything in mental terms cripples the possibility of speaking mysteriously to the deeper levels of human consciousness. As the Church focused more on the control of behavior, it obscured its own somewhat unchartable gift to penetrate the depths of personality.

The results could be observed in a blurring of a sense of what serious sin really was and of a use of the confessional to clear the conscience of what came to be known as imperfections. In certain areas, such as those associated with human sexuality, the experience of guilt was pervasive because there was so little leeway for experiencing sexual feelings of any kind outside the married state. The fundamental unfriendliness toward human feelings has been documented often enough. What is striking is the way in which obsessive mechanisms came to be employed on a large scale in order to handle feelings not only of sexuality but also of anger and a wide range of other emotions. This is the heart of the Catholic psychological conflict. The obsessive keeping of rules or following the instructions of others on how to live provided a way of handling the anxiety about one's behavior that would otherwise necessarily arise. At its most intense form this obsessiveness was revealed in scrupulosity; in its milder versions in the slight mistrusting of the self that characterized the experience of many Catholics. It could be found also in the brooding melancholy of more sensitive persons who were existentially dissatisfied with their continuing failure to meet what were sometimes bizarre self-imposed standards of behavior. To live in view of the expectations of others estranged many Catholics from a sense of themselves. This has been the theme of a thousand rueful Catholic recollections; they resembled children experiencing the famous "double bind" of conflicting parental expectations: Don't sin, but I have the power to forgive you. And, oh, yes, come home before you die.

This led not only to the use of frankly obsessive mechanisms like the repetition of ejaculations in order to keep one's thoughts and feelings in line but also to a hesitancy about investing in or enjoying fully this life. The bags must remain packed and our resources must be saved rather than spent because a long journey was yet to be made. This attitude of not being able to let go, of holding back, of not being able to spend one's affectional or spiritual capital for fear that there would be none at some later and vaguer time was not uncommon among those who experienced the Catholic culture. It was given words in Eugene O'Neill's famous *Long Day's Journey into Night,* as the father, the old Irish actor James Tyrone, stands up to tighten a lightbulb he had previously loosened in order to economize. It is a revelation of one fearful and unresolved Catholic style. Tyrone's wife, formerly in the convent, is a drug addict; one son is an alcoholic, the other tubercular. The old man pauses, "What was it, I wonder, that I wanted to buy that was worth . . . ? Well, no matter, it's a late day for regrets. . . . No, I can't remember what the hell it was I wanted to buy. . . ." I have heard that groan a countless number of times from Catholics who had denied themselves something of their lives and no longer felt free to reclaim; from those who were struggling with the feeling that they could never quite please themselves or anyone else; with somewhat sad and restless people ready to believe in anything but themselves.

It is clear that this obsessive conflict may reflect only one period of Catholic experience and that it is no longer the problem it once was but, I submit, it is undeniable that it affected many American Catholics whose religious environment was shared by what one writer called "postfamine, west of Ireland spirituality." It may have blunted the creative possibilities of many persons caught in this conflict. The present reaction against rules of all kinds—the dramatic rejection of institutional authority—the search for different gurus: These are not unrelated to the long, chill night of Catholic obsessiveness.

Other aspects of Catholic experience invite our attention. There is another side to this ambivalence toward human beings, a quality never extinguished by the obsessive conflict. This was a residual compassion for the human condition, a willingness to suspend the rules that was built, through epikeia and Canon 209, into the very rules themselves. This potent sense of solidarity with imperfect man has been preserved in its people, in the living tradition of its ministers and its members. What could sound strict and unbending in the abstract would almost always be more forgiving and understanding in the concrete. This willingness to understand frailty and to view the human struggle with unaffected tenderness has also been part of the Catholic inheritance. The Church possesses some awareness of all the history through which it has lived; it is, in a sense, the Here Comes Everybody of *Finnegan's Wake*. That is part of what has made the Church fascinating even in its failures and why it cannot be easily dismissed from one's imagination. It is the reason that so many of those who have lived in it experience ambivalent feelings—as they would toward an imperfect parent—of irritation and affection, of bitterness and longing toward it, of why some want to get out of it and then miss it, of why its experience of the tree of Eden and the tree of Calvary, fall-redemption, and death-resurrection resonate still. A People of God; Here Comes Everybody, indeed.

The Church survives also as the nourisher of the unconscious, as the great reservoir of myth and symbol that provides interpretations of life far more subtly and far more surely than rules or laws ever do. The creative Church, one might call it, the existential and poetic aspect of the Church that has never submitted fully to rules and that has been the source of symbols for so much of Western history. It is this Church that awakens men to life: the authentic underground Church that cannot speak except in myths and symbols; the unconscious Church that speaks to the unconscious of the race. It fits, to some extent, what Jung once said of the unconscious:

We might call it a collective human being combining the characteristics of both sexes, transcending youth and age, birth and death . . . he would be a dreamer of age-old dreams and, owing to his immeasurable experience, would be an incomparable prognosticator. He would have lived countless times over the life of the individual, of the family, tribe and people, and he would possess the living sense of the rhythm of growth, flowering and decay.[1]

[1] *Modern Man in Search of a Soul* (New York: Harcourt, Brace & Company, 1956), p. 215.

The Church has been hooked into the dynamics of human development at a level that it does not fully understand. It has a poetic function in history that at times it has attempted to disown or repress. Indeed, it has muffled it frequently in its massive efforts to impose an intellectual understanding on aspects of human behavior—like believing—that cannot be summed up or understood with complete success in this way. It has tapped into history and responds with all the genius of its mythical intuition and its profound religious language of symbols. In its efforts to be literal it has diminished its own poetic power. It is somewhat out of touch with this side of its being and does not at times recognize its own richness. This symbolic power is, however, one of the reasons that it can speak beyond all logic to the hearts of its members.

The declaration of the dogma of the Assumption may be a case in point. While insisting on a literal acceptance of the dogma and buttressing this with a variety of rational arguments, the Church was also speaking a symbolic language that it no longer understood. That is why Jung counted the declaration as the most significant religious action of the century; he could hear and see the image that the Church was offering to mankind. It was something from the Church's own unconscious, a powerful symbolization at the dawn of the space age of mother earth returning to the heavens. The dawning age would see, of course, that the heavens and earth could no longer be divided against each other, that the earth was *in* the heavens, and that a new era of understanding about the unity of the universe had begun. A not unreligious insight because of its implications for the unity of human experience as well.

The Eucharist may be a classic example of a powerful ritual that spoke to all levels of human personality—that fairly teemed with what scientists call "surplus" meaning— and that may have been diminished through modernizing it into the vernacular. The reasons, of course, have been good, but the changes may have been built on an intellectual conviction that a Eucharist more understandable intellectually would be more effective. It does stand to reason. But, of course, symbols transcend reason, and the extraordinary grace of the Latin Mass—along with its power to speak to us viscerally—was not totally appreciated in the liturgical renewal. The liturgy is not an area for rationality; it is where the poetic Church touches us with profound sacramental power. It is the sphere outside time in which we believe with our total selves. It may be too early for second questions about the liturgical renewal, but they are bound to arise, and the Latin Mass may reappear before the century ends. It will be a return not to dead tradition but to living religious experience.

What does the reality of Catholic experience mean to many sensitive persons at the present time? Joseph Campbell anticipated the struggle several years ago as he contrasted Protestant symbolic impoverishment with what was then a different condition for Catholics:

The plight of the Catholic, on the other hand, is today precisely the opposite. For he is not deprived; he is over-laden with symbols which have been built into his very nerves but have no relevance to modern life; and his dangerous exposure, therefore, is not to a void within, but, as a kind of Rip van Winkle or perennial Don Quixote, to an alien world without, which in his heart is dogmatically denied and is yet, to his eyes, visible before him . . . if the walls of the Church break apart—as they had for many already in the Middle Ages—he has literally Hell to pay. His problem then is either to liquidate to himself the structuring mythology of his mythologically structured life, or else somehow to unbind its archetypical symbols from their provincial Christian, pseudo-historic references and restore them to their primary force and value as mythological-psychological universals—which in fact has been the typical effort of unorthodox Catholic thinkers in the West ever since the military victory of Constantine and the enforcement, then, by Theodosius the Great of one incredible credo for the Western World.[2]

The present crisis of Catholic experience centers on the mythic dissociation that has taken place. The Catholic world no longer holds together quite as it once did. It is not surprising that, in view of our need for mythic renewal, theologians have rediscovered narrative. The task, however, is not to force our theologians to become storytellers but to free them and encourage them to rediscover the unconscious life of the Church, to learn to speak its many languages and to understand its varied symbols once more. It is a time for theologians to sense all the theology that lies in poetry rather than to try to force all their theology into poetic terms. It is a difficult time of liberation and rediscovery, of experiencing Catholicism in a way that transcends but does not destroy the rational. We all meet at the tree of Eden and the tree of Calvary, in fall-redemption and death-resurrection. Here Comes Everybody.

[2] *The Masks of God: Creative Mythology* (New York: The Viking Press, 1970), pp. 368–69.

2

The End of Romantic America

The words have been shouted, but the poetry is yet to be written about the enormous changes that have taken place over the past decade. The fragments whirl but they are not clearly in focus yet; still we share a feeling that something has happened to us, something whose uncharted shape balloons out in the darkness beyond the hard edges of our daily experience. We know that things have changed and the world we once knew is a ghost, a phantom for nostalgic longing. We even see the Depression years through a gauzy lens that makes them romantic. Perhaps because romance, our American romance with life and love and progress, is the thing that died on us.

Many social observers date the death of romantic America at the assassination of the President in Dallas in 1963. Interpretations vary, but there is little doubt that John Kennedy's death marked the end of what seemed like a new and hopeful beginning for America, a tiny wedge of time made of the stuff of hope, of promises not yet kept, of dreams as yet unrealized, of something never fully tested about what we might have been. It is also clear that we do not yet understand the meaning of the death of the President; we are not yet done with our mourning. We keep talking about it because we have not yet said the last word about it. It has not been incorporated into our national experience nor integrated into our personal histories. It is too big, too complex in its symbolism, and too crushing in its implications to check off and have done with easily. It may one day be looked on as the end of a long period of naïve innocence about the nature of our country's institutions and the purity of our motives and goals.

We have had enormous difficulty letting go of Camelot. It has not been easy to accept a new realism about our politics, education, and churches precisely because they depend upon a certain amount of illusion—call it healthy mystique—in order to function effectively. "Tell the truth," an old professor of mine once said, "but not too much." It is difficult to absorb and make our own the truths that have been doggedly unveiled during the past ten years. We have been dizzied by the Vietnam experience, the Watergate phenomenon, the shaky ethical sensibilities of many formerly unquestioned professions, and the seeming collapse of the power of moral persuasion on the part of the Church. We feel our frustrations keenly because it is so difficult to define, respond, or even blame anybody for the situation in which we find ourselves. It is small wonder that there is such bitter conflict between our old ideals and our new sense of reality, between what we once believed in with conviction and simplicity and what we hesitate to believe in because of its complexity and lack of attractiveness.

We have come to the end of the romantic way of looking at ourselves as Americans. Alistair Cook may remind us of our best instincts in his televised observations about American history but, for the moment at least, we are hardly as self-congratulatory as we once were about the glories of

our democracy. If we have yielded up a romantic interpretation of the American experience, we have not yet
achieved a new sense of our collective or individual meanings. Meaning escapes many persons because we are not
sure what we believe in nor what we can still become. We
are, if anything, trying to hold on until a better day. Good
news has been as short as energy lately; our once-proud
flags seem to be at half mast. Even the once thrilling sounds
melancholy now.

The age has invited disillusionment with almost everybody and everything. Nothing works right, nothing is made
right, and few institutions or individuals seem heroic in our
eyes. We may have suffered from too many exposés; we
have, in some sectors of life at least, experienced from an
almost suicidal tendency to beat our breasts and feel guilty.
It is an emotion not without foundation. Perhaps the
saddest symbol of our disillusionment with public figures
was that of the resigned Agnew explaining to the nation on
television that he would not have been left naked to his
enemies except for the emergence of a new, post-Watergate
morality. And Nixon incapable of even a last moral utter-
ance as he left office. Such morally adolescent translations
of "I'm only guilty because I was caught" make it difficult
for any age group to trust or even like the leadership it has
elected. Richard Nixon's own squirming efforts to survive
for his own sake rather than for the sake of his country
engendered even less cheer. Indeed, it was possible for
even a casual observer to note during the Watergate period
that the concern of the indicted was not so much with right
and wrong as it was with the manipulation of the appearance of right and wrong. It was no accident that the legal
profession suddenly emerged in the public consciousness
as having made a fine art of destroying justice in the name
of legal niceties. Add to the long list of disgraced government officials the public dis-ease with the phenomena of

profiteering doctors, vanishing clergymen, and robber baron oil executives, and one can sympathize with the generalized American "staring reaction," the kind of fixed looks found in groups of people in shock after a traumatic experience.

What romantic excitement existed in religion was largely found in the Catholic Church which, caught up in a massive effort to renew itself, spawned hope and enthusiasm unknown in it for centuries. Suddenly, after generations of unquestioned duty, Catholics became intoxicated with the idea of being able to lead freer lives. They were soon to find that the fact of leading a freer life was much more difficult than the idea of leading a freer life. A hint of revolutionary vitality was in the post-Vatican II air, and it found its most dramatic and conflicted expression in what has been termed the New Catholic Left, the now dispersed band of priests, nuns, and religious brothers who stood out as protesters against the Vietnam War. "Revolution," Dan Berrigan once said in a television interview, "is ecstasy." He meant that revolution delivered the experience in which one could stand out from the ordinary and know the exhilaration of the heightened moments of personal witness in the public forum. The New Catholic Left, which, in fact, was built on sturdy traditional consciences, is no more. Its symbolic end may well have been the marriage of Philip Berrigan and Elizabeth McAllister, an event which, to many of their admirers, seemed a betrayal of the kind of hope that their essential vision of Christian reality had once inspired.

The larger New Left Movement is also shattered, its leaders dispersed and its constituency nonexistent. The campuses have become so quiet that one professor in Florida recently noted, "If you liked the fifties, you'll love the seventies," a shorthand description of the return of somnolence to most college and university settings. In the meantime, however, the appearance of radically changed lifestyles on the campus and in the lives of young adults has persisted. A sexual revolution supposedly took place in America during the sixties, and it left many of our moral convictions and practices in ruins. Aside from the debate about the origin, extent, and implications of the so-called sexual revolution, there is little doubt that people feel that it has taken place and that attitudes toward traditional moral concepts like marriage and fidelity seem to have changed markedly. People talk as though they had changed, and it has become difficult to enunciate any moral propositions that would seem to hold in any reliable but consistent manner on these subjects. There may, in fact, be some moral question about how trends and events are communicated to the American public and whether such transmission, under the pressures of its own deliverance, accurately or faithfully informs people about what is taking place in their country. It becomes the eye of the journalist, whether print or electronic, through which we see our world. The media and their effect on our perceptions have also become subjects of conflict. There are, however, very few facts or studies about the nature of our informational processes and the elements that may tend to introduce distortion in them. We react not necessarily to what is there but to what we think we see.

The media had a hand in publicizing the new trends in sexual identification. The year 1974 saw a rapid crest in the public profession of bisexuality, the new badge of being *in* that has caused conflict on many levels of society. Bisexuality has, for example, become a potent political weapon in the hands of various liberation movements. It has seemed to be the solution to the uncertain gender identity experienced by many young persons on campuses. It has, in the debate within the American Psychiatric Association, revealed how doctors can disagree on the implications of homosexuality.

Perhaps the public would expect doctors to disagree on something about which so little is known. What has become peculiarly embarrassing to the influence and authority of psychiatry in general has been the mode of changing the designation in the official diagnostic manual of homosexuality from an illness to a disturbance of sexual orientation. This action was taken by the board of directors of the American Psychiatric Association without consultation with its members, many of whom took sharp issue with making such a change under what seemed to them the pressures of the Gay Liberation Movement more than scientific validity. A referendum was initiated and a vote was scheduled in order to allow the psychiatrists of the country to express themselves to the board of directors on the matter. In what can only remind one of the late Nixon government's efforts to make everything look right no matter what was really taking place underneath, the board of directors dispatched a letter to all the member psychiatrists cautiously expressing their anxiety about how it would look if the membership sharply disagreed with the decision they had made. It was not given much publicity, and even though the board of directors was sustained by the vote, there has seldom been an embarrassment of such proportions in any professional society. It reflects as well as anything the general confusion that is a common American experience in trying to understand and speak about serious issues.

This was paralleled by the conflicts within the Churches about the question of the morality of homosexual activity, homosexual marriages, and the admission of practicing homosexuals to the sacramental life of the Church itself. Conflicting pastoral guidelines, for example, emerged early in 1974 from the National Conference of Catholic Bishops and from the National Federation of Priests' Councils. There is little comfort in realizing that confusion reigns not only in ecclesiastical but also in scientific realms as well.

There is no question that the Catholic Church's teaching authority which, among most of the churches, remained forceful and influential until very recent times, took a serious battering in the wake of the discussion and investigations that followed Paul VI's reassertion of the traditional Catholic teaching on birth control. The discussion is too familiar to recount, but the issuance of the Encyclical may prove also to have been a symbolic movement in the history of the Catholic Church. It may have been a moment in which the Church's capacity to enunciate a credible ideal and thus to command obedience dissolved. Many who agree with the ideal proposed by the Pope feel that his failure to incorporate a greater understanding for ordinary human experience made him the classic symbolic Church leader who lives at a comfortable distance from everyday life. This discussion, with its implications for the formation of conscience, the meaning of moral ideals, and the Church's teaching authority, has not yet ended. There is, however, no doubt that many Catholics have come to identify themselves in a broader and more ecumenical fashion. They perceive themselves as Christians in the Catholic tradition, which gives them a great deal more freedom of movement than they enjoyed when they felt that their religious identity was caught in an enclosed circle of absolute loyalty to the Church and its literal teachings. Christians have clearly become liberated to some degree from their former rigid adherence to Church teaching. This has not been without its price, however, in terms of the alienation and loneliness many of them feel at being separated in this way from the Church. It is a testimony to the harshness of the times.

This phenomenon has also contributed to the deromanticizing of the Catholic Church as the traditional and unchanging monolithic structure that was able to live outside of time and culture because it tapped its roots into eternity. The Church has turned out to be as human as any other

religious institution, and yet its once powerful influence in
instructing and in directing persons in their personal lives has
been shattered. It is simply not respected or trusted as it
once was. The most touching evidence of this lies in the
anguish that good and talented priests have recently experienced when they have been informed that they might be
called upon to become bishops. These men do not dislike
the Church, but they are keenly aware of the conflict that
they would experience if they were publicly asked to support teachings about moral issues that they feel are behind
the times and out of tune with a basic gospel interpretation
of the Christian life.

The end of the romantic period of renewal in the Catholic
Church has also, somewhat paradoxically, brought an end
to the sharply critical attitudes that were given such free
expression in the post-Vatican II era. It is not exactly that
people agree with the old-fashioned Church as much as
that they see little profit, either institutionally or personally,
from continued attacks on an organization that they still perceive with a mixture of affectionate respect and regret. The
reasons for this are complex, but ordinary people realize
that there is a point at which criticism becomes markedly
unproductive. Not only is it ineffective, but it also drains so
much from the spirit of the attackers that it does more harm
to them than good to the institutions. Too many people have
been hurt in the religious wars of the past few years to continue a battle that can only lead to a compromise truce
rather than to complete victory. If the institutional Church
cannot be totally defeated, neither can it completely de-
feat anybody anymore; this represents a loss of power that
threatens a loss of an old identity.

People can walk away from the Church and feel that they
have not really left it; priests, barred from any thought of
such a move for years, can now freely seek dispensation from
their commitments and return to the lay life, in which they

may continue as practicing Catholics. The presumed sexual revolution has also had a strong effect on the way in which Catholics have evaluated their own previously highly restrictive attitudes toward sexuality inside and outside of marriage. All these things can take place without the necessity of a continual barrage of heavy ordinance at the Vatican. Changes continue to occur, but they are not being enunciated as dramatically as during the romantic period of Catholic Church renewal. Many Christians also feel a certain chill at the idea of separating themselves totally from the institution in which they were reared and that houses so many of the symbols and traditions that have marked and defined their lives. They are not anxious—even though this evaluation may take place at an unconscious level—to rid themselves of the canopy of symbols under which they have lived their lives. They stick with the Church in some kind of relationship; they want to believe, but faith is not as easy or as automatic as it once was.

We have entered what might be termed the era of hard questions. These center on ourselves, the nature of religion, the source of possible meaning for our existence, and the moral guidelines that offer a credible direction for our everyday lives. Aside from the theological discussions that must be conducted within the limitations of scholarly discipline, common men and women want to know how they can and should lead their lives. This is not because of the pressure of obsessiveness but from some deep feeling that there are things that can be defined as right or wrong, and that they would like to take account of them in their judgments about their lives and actions. The subjects that concern them center on themselves and their own identity as well as their relationships with the community in which they live. They touch on such diverse questions as sexuality, politics, and what it means to do a day's work. When most of our familiar institutions seem caught up in a cultural change that has shaken their confidence and their capacity to lead and teach, the average person still has genuine questions about the parameters of their lives and destinies. In some ways, the question comes down to this: Is there such a thing as common-sense morality? Is there not some way, if God is not a deceiver, to discern what is proper in his eyes that also fits human nature? Can't this be done without convoluting things so that even the idea of right and wrong seems to disappear?

There must be, ordinary people feel, some sensible middle ground between the traditional, tight-fisted view of morality and the new amorphous humanism which, in its manifesto about life, seems more concerned about contraception, abortion, and euthanasia than anything else. If the original morality trivialized the events of life, seeding them with enough moral distinctions to harvest pervasive and unmanageable guilt, naïve new movements—like the wide-eyed human potential movement—offer a flawed and unsatisfying romanticism about life and morality. We live, however, in a postromantic age. The questions are hard, the issues are urgent, and men and women are troubled about their incapacity to come to grips with them. Sin seems to have disappeared. Now ambiguity is celebrated, and, in faith, politics, and sex, the guides seem as confused and the pathways all overgrown.

It is the fashion these days to be glowingly optimistic or terribly pessimistic about our future chances, a range of attitudes that has been applied to everything from nuclear war to family life. We are either getting much worse or getting much better. The middle ground, however, is where most people live. They are deceived by rhetoric that supposedly stops trends, or urges them to the latest avante-garde behavioral expressions. They question whether adjustment is the same as morality, whether a somnolent balance is the proper condition for human existence. Has the therapeutic ideal triumphed, as many observers say, over an old tradition of morality? Listening carefully one understands that, beneath the confusion and the strange metaphysical pain that they cannot quite define, many common people are searching for a new moral sense. They have been instructed in leading the good life, but not far below their consciousness they are more concerned about the right life. They want their gift of life to display purpose and to give evidence of meaning. They would like some answers at a time when the death of the romantic in American life has left them strangers on a road where they once thought they knew the way.

3

A Sense of Life

It is a tragedy of some contemporary techniques that instead of leading us to wisdom's gates they confuse and estrange us from it. A second cousin, perhaps, to the problem of why so many people who are manifestly unfit for classrooms manage to get into the teaching profession and to make their pupils almost permanent enemies of ordered learning. We are awash in statistics and graphs that tell us all about twentieth-century life but make it harder for us to know what it means to be alive. It may be a symptom that we are hypnotized by the *Guinness Book of World Records*, that magnificent collection of mostly trivial accomplishments that diverts us but hardly furthers our understanding of the existence it measures in snippets. A predilection for counting has made the social scientist an easy target for those who understand that the human person can never be described satisfactorily in digits. Other approaches to knowledge have had a better press, but they also alienate us from the human sense of purpose that they are meant to deliver.

This includes, unfortunately, some of the methodologies

associated with theology. It is clear that theology is not the same as religion, but it has had a powerful role in shaping the conscience of Western man and blessing or blighting his undertakings and possibilities. The point of these observations is not to criticize theology as much as to observe the constraints under which, until very recently, it has labored. A narrow approach in moral theology meant that all life and behavior had to be analyzed as either good or bad according to one acceptable school of thought. One of the problems of contemporary moral theology—but a healthy one—is associated with the efforts of sensitive practitioners to come to terms with a plurality of methods in assaying the issues of human morality. One can sympathize and strongly support the efforts of theologians to move into modern times with a greater openness to different conceptualizations and styles of theologizing. Unfortunately, while they move at their necessarily scholarly pace, ordinary people stand in what seems the lengthening shadows of the very twilight of morality itself.

The average man or woman has very little interest in the technical aspects of theologizing. That is why theology runs the risk of being an alienating rather than an integrating force as they perceive it in their lives. I am not referring now to bitter or rebellious people, but rather to the throngs of conscientious and caring individuals who do indeed want to live their lives with a feeling of wholeness and rightness. They already experience bewilderment and frustration about finding adequate moral guideposts. They are estranged from the practical challenges that confront them every day by theologians who debate in their own special language about a variety of ethical traditions. Ordinary people have more basic difficulties, and they want answers—or at least a practical way of deriving answers for themselves —about how to manage their moral choices in life. An abstract morality alienates them because it appears to be removed from the myriad challenges that are connected with the human experiences that are most significant and important to them. They want an informed and serious way to understand and handle life because it matches their restless longings as well as their immediate concerns. What, they wonder, does it mean to be alive?

This fundamental moral question is not an easy one, not in a world with so many potent symbolic interpretations of life. The roots of meaning seem to be different on the subcontinent of India where, committing themselves to the reality of reincarnation, the people find it difficult to be as concerned as outside observers about the incredible poverty and hunger that is elevated to a new power each year by an exploding birth rate. Not only the answer but the question is different for many Americans who lives now at a great distance from the inconvenient, Depression-ridden thirties. The meaning of life for a great number has been associated with success, with getting on, with a constantly growing economy and a correlated growth in the sense of one's own importance and influence. Within this cultural setting many Christians have revised their own viewpoint on existence over the past decade.

Catholics in particular have shifted from a long-range view of history, which for centuries had counted the immediate things of life as inconsequential compared to the reward that awaited the faithful in heaven. This potent religious view included a tendency to postpone justice and to defer happiness until a later date, when the moral books would be audited anew and our souls would be cleansed of the impurities gathered during our earthly lives. It was a remarkably functional world view. Under it people made enormous sacrifices to the extent of surrendering, in many cases, even the chance of discovering their own true personalities. This symbolic taking of another name for religious was merely one symbol of the way that this ideal could recruit people into anonymous legions whose boast was that they had surrendered all claims to themselves in this life. There was something staggeringly attractive about the absolute nature of this kind of commitment. But one can hardly deny that it also led to a certain distance from and at least an occasional failure in responsibility in regard to immediate world problems.

There are those who hesitate to separate Catholics too much from what they conceive to be the eschatological concerns inherent in this viewpoint. Some people feel that the Catholic tradition has been so associated with a larger view of reality that too intense a concern with the present world—or even with one's own life—might destroy a very rich value. The tension that makes the issue tremble merely singles out the fact that a heartfelt and significant question about the Catholic tradition of life has just come to be asked. We cannot waiver in its first formulation; it is too good a beginning. What does the Catholic tradition point to about life? How indeed are Catholics to be distinctive in the way they regard themselves or their neighbors? Such questions tell us that we have begun not only to take ourselves but also our own religious beliefs seriously enough to investigate them in order to sort out what is alive from what is dead, what is moral from what is not.

Unless we take ourselves seriously as human beings, we cannot be moral or Christian at all. Taking oneself seriously as a person is not the same as regarding oneself solemnly or narcissistically. It means digging into one's existence, acknowledging the mystery of consciousness, and exploring the dimensions of one's own personality with a mixture of acuity and tenderness, with an attitude of compassionate confrontation. *Primum vivere*, the great saying went, and it might now be translated that the first thing we have to have is a sense of what it means to be alive.

It is a sad fact that, in the name of morality and virtue,

many people have led "correct" but cramped and highly priced lives. These people may never have done anything wrong, but they may never have decided anything for themselves either. Too many of them have lived with the shadows of fear almost blotting out the experience of love in their lives. They have existed with a tight control over passion, but such intense restraint was sometimes deadly to their human identity. It is not surprising that many people, believing that their superiors or teachers really knew what they were doing, threw themselves into the pursuit of virtue with a wild readiness to pluck out the offending eye or to sever the potentially sinful limb. Nor is it surprising that many of these same people grew restless with a pain that they could not name; they had given up a lot of their own lives, and they could not help but feel the ache. It was like the "phantom" limb reported by people after surgical removal of a leg or an arm. They can still feel pain in it; that is the kind of pain that many people, caught up in a cultural and religious context that pressed them for singleminded virtue, knew in their own lives. Their assent to somebody else's plans for their actions often meant that they never really came to terms with their own truth or with their own lives.

Other persons not so self-consciously religious or so solemnly committed to certain styles of the spiritual life have lived freer but far more mistake-laden lives. Their lives are not orderly, but they bear the marks of their own individuality. They have had an identity and, readily acknowledging their sinfulness, have at least been in touch with themselves and with others in the process of struggling with life. They have not been heroically virtuous, but they had been heroically alive. Are they the sinners or the truly holy people?

I have always felt that if you could look closely enough at people, if you could get deep down enough into their lives and motivations, you could never get mad at them. You would be able to read the strange signals of their more bizarre moments and so make sense of them at last. You could then feel for their problems and restrain the tendency to judge them harshly. In fact, a close look at human beings leads us to question our eagerness to assign moral fault or virtue on the basis of superficial observations. Inevitably, a close examination of people's lives would give birth to a basic compassion for them. Just such a feeling colors the observations of this book. It does not suggest that there is no such thing as right or wrong; the point is that we must take people seriously enough to look deeply within them, and we cannot be put off by a quick glance at externals. To approach human persons tenderly is not the same thing as approaching them romantically. We must land somewhere on this side of the steamy baths of fulfillment at Essalen in the world where ordinary persons struggle and make mistakes and fall and get up again in pursuit of the truth about themselves.

It is not a small accomplishment to sense that one has participated in existence in some depth. When we speak of a right to life we must include some opportunity to understand that we are alive. The very simplicity of the phrase almost defeats its statement. The sad fact is that this basic right to life is denied to many, distorted for still others, and only painfully realized for many beyond that. It is difficult for many persons to grasp even dimly a sense of what it means to be a person, to taste existence both in its joys and its disappointments, and to run the risks that go into being human. But is there any other way to lead a moral life?

This is related to the many movements presently aimed at raising human consciousness about various aspects of what it means to be a person. Perhaps the most obvious movement connected with that centers on the meaning of being a woman. It is no less applicable to an awareness of what it means to be a man. So too the theology of liberation sounds its battle cries in order to challenge those forces that make basic self-realization so difficult for millions of oppressed individuals. These consciousness-raising movements proceed on different paths and at various levels, but all of them, in imperfect and incomplete ways, work to the same purpose. They remind us that it is difficult for men and women to appreciate their humanity unless they have the space, freedom, and encouragement to do this. Taking oneself seriously is particularly difficult if we live in a culture or a tradition where blind forces have operated over an extended period to make this difficult if not impossible. Fascism in national and ecclesiastical environments has made it easier to obey the will of another than to discover the meaning of oneself. To deny people the chance for moral awakening may be the unforgivable sin, because it goes against the spirit of life itself.

If oppression seems a deliberate sin, then the capacity to distract people from the basic issues of their existence contains just as much potential for evil. Indeed, we have built a culture of distractions in which our technology has raised the possibilities of leading a shallow and unfocused life to new heights. All of this makes getting acquainted with oneself and one's possibilities and opportunities ever more remote. People need not look at themselves when they can look at television or pursue the dreamy "good" life without ever coming across a hint about their own deep identity.

What do people want or need in order to be and experience themselves as human beings? This is not a question posed to rid us of the defective or the crippled, of those some glibly judge as unable to experience life fully. Indeed, many of these have an intense sense of what it means to be alive, one far richer than that of people who are unpenalized by nature or fortune in any way. This is not to suggest, in other words, that we are trying to create a master race in which genetic engineering will fill streets and lanes only with those fair of face and form. Making it possible for persons to experience life deeply is a much simpler notion, which is built on providing people with the chance to sense their own individuality. This is an important opportunity—the only one they have—to face their own life honestly. Even if they do not do this completely, they will at least have encountered the elements from which the meaning of their existence is constructed. People have a basic moral right to live in the circumstances in which they can come to grips with themselves. It is clear that society's institutions must struggle to establish and support these liberating conditions and, in every possible way, to validate the existence of each individual person.

A complicated moral issue centers on the need for the kind of co-operation and informed ethical vision needed to create the environment in which more people can penetrate their own lives more freely and more fully. Talking about this can unfortunately make something that is essential sound like the pie-in-the-sky promises one finds scattered across the human potential movement, the *Reader's Digest*, and "The Waltons" television series. Experiencing life in enough depth to earn some scars from it is far different from the dreamy visions of such entrepreneurs of human personality. Letting people find themselves does not depend on the manipulation of persons by positive thinking, energized will power, or any other such hokum.

Why is it hard to take oneself seriously but not solemnly? What is involved in this process? It builds on a sense of identity, a feeling for oneself that is staked out on what is true and reliable about one's gifts, liabilities, and possibilities. A sense of identity means that we have consolidated the elements of ourself in a way that is particular to us, and that it does not depend on borrowings from the outside. The perception of our true selves—a dynamic process that includes an ever-deepening awareness of our continually fresh experience—allows us to see ourselves honestly and fairly. What we see and what we experience with some feeling for our own unity includes a differentiation of our abilities and interests as well as an understanding of our being separate and unique individuals. Our claim to separateness is not made out of rebellion but out of an ever-clear definition of ourselves. This involves taking responsibility for our existence, for writing our own signature on life without hesitation. It is no easy thing to live truthfully and to share ourselves with those around us without undue defensiveness. Experiencing oneself includes taking charge of one's being, of not feeling like a stranger renting out space in the body, nor being a person intimidated by those depths in which bubbling forces move us now this way and now that but into which we never even glance. Experiencing oneself means becoming acquainted with the mystery of one's identity and of being able to live comfortably with it.

Taking ourselves seriously means that we can listen to ourselves. Sometimes we hear just enough to know that we are really not quite ready to understand what we are attempting to say. Our life is filled with such discoveries, of tentative probes, ideas not yet ready to be born, of aspects of ourselves that have not yet come together in some conviction or firm declaration of selfhood. Being a person requires a delicate balance because it is so easy to force oneself into certain postures and by this very act to destroy what has not yet come to life. Listening to ourselves is fundamental in the practical processing of our creativity in everyday life. For most people their primary and fullest experience of creativity will be in relationship to themselves. This involves riding with our growing selves, and learning to wait and be patient, to delay action until we are indeed ready for a moment of personal fullness in which we develop a compassionate but realistic sense of ourselves and so give fuller birth to our personalities. This is a long and slow process but, for the average person, it is essentially connected with morality. Unless our real selves emerge unforced and undisguised, we cannot claim authorship for our own lives or for our relationships or perhaps even for our children or those who are influenced by us in one way or another. They will have been touched by a shadow rather than by a real man or a woman. This is the awesome possibility for those who never get into life in enough depth to make any difference in the lives of others.

I have always had a dreadful vision of the last bomb incinerating the world while half America is watching "Let's Make a Deal" and the other half is listening to Howard Cosell describe a football game. The military, speculating on just such instantaneous communal fates, say that it would happen so suddenly that people would not know what happened to them. The saddest part is that, if they live lives that are trivialized on the magnificent scale available in America, they could survive and still not know what happened to them. Surely there is a moral problem involved in any decision that allows people to be indifferent to their own existence or that leads them to barter away in the name of goals that are beneath their dignity and unsupportive of their true personhood. There is a moral problem seldom enunciated wherever conditions make it more difficult for men and women to sense who they are, or who they can be and what their lives might mean.

So too there is a moral triumph for all those who assist others to lay a richer claim to their own identity and to help them to move a little farther along in understanding and becoming themselves. It must always be remembered that in areas as sensitive as those connected with human growth, a little progress is a lot of progress. The numbing possibility of the age is that, for various reasons, people may miss ever catching a glimpse of the shape of their own existence, so paralyzed are they that their power to be human is trun-

cated or atrophied. Such circumstances yield a harvest of
bitter fruit because we are disinherited, bereft of a sense of
ourselves, and remarkably limited in our capacity to enjoy
life. Joy becomes elusive for those who are never in touch
with themselves. There must be a special hell for all those
persons who deflect people from the opportunity of experiencing their own individual lives, whether these are pos-
sessive parents, meddlesome clerics, manipulating sales
engineers, or politicians with souls paved with the asphalt
of their crooked deals. One has to care about human beings
in order to fight for the opportunities they need to experience themselves in a serious manner.

What, we may ask ourselves, would we be like if we took
our own existence more seriously? We would immediately
be joined to a deeper sense of meaning, a pursuit of purpose
that sometimes escapes us when we look away from or fail
to build the kind of confidence in ourselves we require to
live deeply. We would, were we to judge ourselves as significant, evaluate claims made against us by others in terms
of our own convictions and experience. We would sharpen
our perception of others and be able to separate ourselves
from them so that we could see ourselves and our rights as
distinctly as we can see them and theirs. We would break
through the narcissism that can so encapsulate us and find,
with at least some of our defenses in disarray, that we are at
the edge of a new and more exciting road in life. It would be
a frightening experience, even though it would be the beginning of wisdom for us.

Taking ourselves seriously would involve us immediately
in taking others seriously and not shrugging off our attitudes
or behaviors toward them as of no consequence. It would
mean that we would have to take the world and its problems
seriously and that we would have to stir ourselves in the
name of community concern in order to better the lot of
those with whom we share life. Without this sense of what it

means to be human, morality is only an organizing tyranny that brings us law and order but blinds us and shrivels our moral spirit. Taking ourselves seriously we would find that we are testing and maturing ourselves and our belief systems all the time. We would need to invent no tests because we would find them regularly in the circumstances of our human relationships, productivity, and generativity. They are all around us—our moral universe—but they can only be seen when we have a clear view of ourselves. We might not call it theology, certainly not in our everyday lives, but we would be dealing with the ultimate questions because we could no longer evade them nor hand them over for decision to others around us.

4

A Sense of Sin

Theology, to appropriate Norman Mailer's remark about journalism, is chores. It involves persistent hard work at its own pace and in accord with its own tradition. Part of the current chores of theologians is to deliver a more understandable and practical definition of sin. It is not, of course, that sin has disappeared; old-fashioned ideas about it have vanished, leaving the illusion that sin is no more. Now that the finely engraved tablets of detailed sin have been smashed, we find ourselves in a new and smoky place, a confused and confusing terrain where the tracks of sin tell us that it lives still, that it is an abiding and dominating presence, and that we must look into its face for ourselves.

One can only admire the theologians who have given their energies to the enormously sensitive and difficult task of restructuring moral theology so that it incorporates traditional Christian awarenesses in a respectable modern language. Someday we will recognize the transitional heroism of thinkers like Richard McCormick and Charles E. Curran and their colleagues. They are patient men, and they understand the difficulty of living during what can only be perceived as a gap in the organized presentation of the Christian moral life. What, then, can ordinary persons use in these times to judge themselves and their lives? Not many of them have the talent nor the interest in speculative moral theology; they are concerned with learning how they are to respond to the existential moments in which they must choose one way or the other about themselves, their families, their work, and their obligation to the rest of the human family; what helps them recognize the face of wickedness if they do not have some feeling for the meaning of sin as an enduring operational reality?

A sense of sin is an ancient and respected notion in the Roman Catholic Church, a twitching nerve that has always given proof that the Church was alive, even when that was seriously doubted by most observers. This sense of sin is an inheritance of the Spirit, a bright, flickering aura that has survived the Church's disastrous secular triumphs, its ill-informed self-confidence about truth, and its neurotic legalism. This sense of sin—this awareness of good and evil in practical terms—is related to fundamental gospel attitudes that have always been difficult to get into writing. This enduring impulse in the Church's life has been preserved in the way its people have lived, and in the feeling for the human situation that they have managed to preserve despite all the poisons and mistakes of a troubled ecclesiastical history. A sense of sin is something that lives in the souls of Catholic Christians, and it is powerful enough to preserve their sanity and integrity, to make them the living elements of a Church that survived more truthfully in them than in its institutional structures.

This consciousness of sin is a sign of the action of the Spirit in the lives of men and women. God's promises, after all, are not just promises. One of the ways in which they are realized is in the informed and enduring attitudes that can

be found in the lives of committed believers. This consciousness of our sinful condition does not drape the soul in black
bunting as much as it attunes it to the unretouched reality
of our existence. It is best heard in those persons who strive
to live by the Spirit. It lives also in ancient rituals and
practices through which human sinfulness is acknowledged,
almost embraced, and dealt with straightforwardly. This
consciousness of sin has been a source of energy for Christian
literature and art. Allowing for the distortion of guilt that has
undergirded the Catholic conflict, the sense of sin, at its base,
remains a reliable insight into the way the world works and
the way people meet and relate to each other. It breathes
still in the Catholic culture; it may, like radiation, be deep
in the bones of all those who have grown up in the Church's
shadow. It is not, however, merely a memory but an active
awareness that cannot be dismissed; it echoes in Church
traditions, in the Church's preconscious symbolic life, and in
the Church's identity with its sinful members. An awareness
of sin's power of death has helped to keep the Church alive.

What are the elements of this sense of sin, this miraculous
survivor in Christian history? It includes a mostly unverbalized streetlike wisdom about life itself; it has seen too
much to be naïvely innocent about human possibilities. This
sense of sin recognizes the tragic and brutal elements of
existence, but it also understands that the person is neither
a romantic savage nor a totally corrupt marauder in the universe. Somehow, against all odds, in spite of multiplied mistakes in interpretation, it has preserved some sense of human
beings as a mixture of promise and imperfection, an unfail-
ing intuition about men and women powerful enough even
in small lives to be able to sin. Such insight recognizes that
the person possesses a capacity for evil as well as for good,
that men and women can fail, that there is something risky
about them that makes bad choices a continuing possibility
for them. This is not necessarily a harsh view of humankind;

it is rather an understanding acceptance, a reaching out rather than a rejection of sinners, a willingness to keep in relationship with persons as they make their struggling way through life. Making room for sinners, some sense that the Kingdom of God is strangely but appropriately theirs, is a principal element in the Christian attitude toward good and evil. The Christian sense of sin in the Catholic tradition maintains a sense of balance toward human persons, the kind of knowing appreciation that only those who have struggled with evil can signal to others engaged in their own battles with it.

This understanding of the effort that accompanies a serious Christian life is built on a realization of the stakes that are involved at each choice point in growth. It also acknowledges the way in which life seems continually to test each one of us. There is a dynamic connected with the reality of temptation that involves more than wandering eyes or uncharitable words. The enduring sense of sin puts the entire person into focus by identifying the main issues: Will the person assent to life, negate it, or move back into the shadows of suspended judgment? The sense of sin sharpens our awareness that what we do makes a difference, that our actions have consequences, and that our lives have meaning only if we seriously examine our purpose and motives in the light of Christian values. This acknowledgment of our sinfulness, in other words, situates our basic Christian experience in our everyday lives. Here we take on the flesh of our human situation, confront the challenges through which we find ourselves, and face, if ever we are going to, the mysterious cycle of death and resurrection that is the seal on Christian existence. A lively sense of sin attunes us to what is involved in being a human being; it takes human beings seriously.

This traditional view of men and women is charged with hope because it always raises the possibility of forgiveness and redemption, even in the context of great moral fault or error. This is one of the ways in which the power of resurrection touches believers. We can be forgiven, we can be revived, born again, and our lives are not completely lost, but always ready to be deepened by grace. The sacramental acknowledgment of our sinfulness is a strong element in preserving a sense of sin in the lives of Christians. Penance has operationally translated and summed up essential aspects of living in Christ that could never be preserved in purely theoretical or intellectual terms. The sacramental ritual and reality means that people can do wrong, recognize it, and in God's presence forgive themselves and each other for it. These are the transactions through which we redeem ourselves and each other. Here we touch our own sinfulness in hope rather than despair. We cannot, however, do any of these things unless we break out of ourselves and more deeply into life, a hazardous business at best, a journey on which we might be lost, a journey we are better prepared to make when we have a sense of our own sinfulness.

The sense of sin not only tells us that we know something of the world and its ways, but it also helps us to live more comfortably with this knowledge. The traditional Christian view has not estranged man from his own humanity but has helped him to approach it with greater compassion and understanding. This sense of sin is no stranger to tenderness, and it has always softened the Church's experiential dealings with sinners, even when its official statements have seemed harsh and unforgiving. Perhaps this survival of informed compassion is one of the best and yet least recognized testimonies to the Spirit's guidance of the Church. It has kept something essential in focus, something without which we could never come to terms either with ourselves or with our sinfulness. A living reality, this awareness of sin, a presence that has lived in the soul of Christianity, in some space that has never been crushed by the dead weight of in-

stitutionalization. But it is here, as in the dining room of sinners that Christ is present and where we ourselves are more
fully alive.

This sense of sin, in others words, is not a reasonable
phenomenon, nothing that can be logically analyzed nor
even comfortably theologized over. It radiates on a fine web
of human sensibility in an order of experience very different
from that of elaborated reason. Any attempt to chart the
sense of sin too carefully only makes it more mysterious and
more elusive. That is why it has always been a subject for
poets and novelists. It is not just an instinct or superstition
but a refinement of Christian experience that has been
nurtured in the mystery-filled lives of Christians. The sense
of sin is not a finished product but an incomplete, living
reality. We can only rely, in the long run, on some feeling
for its truth, on an understanding that it matches what we
can understand of our experience when we are serious about
it. An awareness of sin is a gift of the Spirit that belongs to
believers who are maturing in their understanding of themselves, the world, and the human stage on which the drama
of salvation is acted out. We learn a sense of sin through the
self-awareness that is the product of education and of our
individual and social experiences. With a sense of sin we are
prepared for life because we are not desperately innocent in
the face of death.

Included in this sense of the sinful human condition is the
development of a healthy conscience built on traditionally
Christian values but is encouraged to look always more
deeply and more sensitively into itself. The informed Christian conscience does not shut itself off from outside stimula-
tion, but welcomes it. Such a conscience continually grows
through diligent but sympathetic inquiry into the human
situation. A matured conscience is not a tyrant whose demands can never be satisfied. Neither is it a flabby and
permissive attitude that no longer cares what or how things

happen to us. A living conscience cannot be separated from a living person who must learn, ask questions, and seek ever more realistically to determine the morality of life's choices. Its strengthening depends on a true sense of sin.

This kind of growth necessarily involves a man or a woman in a constant examination of their experience. The abiding Christian sense of our sinfulness provides us with a tempered sense of reality that enables us to do this successfully. This vital interaction with the Christian tradition has always placed the person, freedom, and the rights of others in a prominent position in our deliberations. It is not an intellectual exercise but a genuine experience of the mystery of living in and with Jesus, and it looks more ordinary than people might expect. There are no bells ringing, no fanciful tongues being spoken; we experience it as we make ourselves present in the moments of decision through which we can truly own and be responsible for what we do. It is a practical way of enabling us to take ourselves seriously as human beings.

This sense of sin does not mean that we are overcome by it or lost under its black weight. Opposite to it is the grim view that we are incapable of any good on our own. The texture of Christian personality may be uneven, but it contains elements of strength and a capacity to respond in a positive and wholehearted way. The drama of our existence is worked out in this process of bringing ourselves to life as we choose for or against our own greater fullness. At important points of decision we either make more of ourselves present in life or we cut off that possibility; we put ourselves, to some extent, to death. A sense of sin acquaints us with this reality just as it acquaints us with our own limits and forces us to sort out our motives and to listen carefully to the messages that come from our own depths. Persons who take themselves seriously discover new aspects of themselves in the kinds of experiences that are intensely human. They find life and moral choice in the common issues of friendship, love, and trust. Although their failures give them scars, they also feel the validation of their own existence that comes from being actively involved with the questions of personal good and evil. The battle is not cosmic for most of us; it looks as common as our everyday existence.

Persons who take themselves seriously are able to discover who they are and what they can do in and with life. Normally they do this in social settings in which they recognize the boundaries of their own personalities and in which they make increasing room for the personalities of others. Believers are alive when they break out of their own heads, when they stop abstractly thinking about life and to live it in its temptations and challenges, in the decisions through which they define their integrity. The test comes to this: Are we going to be present in life or not? Can we see more deeply into existence because of the truths given to us in the teachings of Jesus? Are we going to take the meaning of our lives seriously or distract ourselves endlessly instead? Are we going to discover the significance at all? Do we perceive the discrete events of our existence as full of the potential of good and evil, as well as of the promise of redemption and resurrection? Or are we blind to the realities in which we are involved every day, dull to a sense of sin and lost therefore to any profound sense of life?

We are the captors of sin when we fail to confront the fact that we make a difference in the world in which we live. The first difference, of course, is to ourselves; it hinges on whether we ever find out who we are and take seriously our obligation to bring as much of ourselves into life as we can. The sinner, according to the old phrase of Aquinas, "does not love himself enough." His fundamental failure is to himself. It is a failure of presence, a failure of awareness of oneself and the persons all around us in life. This failure to define and so to separate oneself from other persons makes the worthwhile experiences of life almost inaccessible. Perhaps people who never get out of themselves are more sinned against than sinning, but this only points to the seriousness with which we must take life and our responses to other persons. It is clear that we can cripple and take the possibility of life itself away from them—and so estrange them from the possibility of ever even accurately understanding the difference between good and evil, of tasting life or not for themselves.

The terrible consequences of moral dullness are found in the lives of those for whom everything is neutral or in whose personality the impulse to be concerned about truth or other values can barely be felt. These persons have never discovered their true selves, and so they cannot operate from inside; they can only be moved by outer pressures, but they never know what it means to experience existence —and moral responsibility for it—from within.

These persons are cut off from the Spirit because they are cut off from any real feeling for themselves. They are isolated from the Gospel impulse when their hardheartedness is defined by their inability to receive or to transmit the vital messages of life. This deadness of the heart makes it difficult for such persons to hear or to sense other people in their lives. It is difficult for them to make moral judgments because they cannot hear their neighbors' voice, nor can they separate it from their own concern.

The inheritor of a sense of sin is not without a basis for judgment even when moral theology has not yet provided new and definite guidelines about the choices of life. He or she is acquainted with the important things in life; they are present to life. In a concrete sense they are there responding with love to others and taking responsibility for their daily decisions. These people have a center of gravity that enables them to feel—or to have an instinct for—what is right or wrong. They can test this against the resonations of the

Spirit within them. They know whether this action will add to or detract from themselves. They sense its implications for other persons and, often without any elaborate or conscious reasoning, they know deeply what is right or wrong. They have learned to listen to themselves and to trust what is right and healthy inside of themselves. This feeling is not unbridled emotionally but the kind of adult reactivity that is always found in responsible persons. It is the sign that we are present in life, that we understand it and take it on its own terms. We love ourselves enough to feel our own existence, and we know that we are not alone, that we live with others, and are caught up with them in the mystery of sin and forgiveness. We can make our way together because we recognize ourselves as sinners filled with the hope and promise of redeeming each other.

5

A Sense of Values

Our real selves lie behind the things we value, the things we strive for, the things we save, the persons and causes to which we make some kind of enduring commitment. "A value," according to psychologist Gordon W. Allport, "is a belief upon which a man acts by preference."[1] Milton Rokeach, the psychologist who has spent twenty-five years studying human values, believes that they are a special kind of belief, "a prescriptive or proscriptive belief."[2] Our values issue into action, into the behavior that forms the outline of our existence and that, implicitly at least, gives what Victor Frankl once referred to as an "account for the purpose of our existence." Values are not, then, merely abstract ideals but the concepts that govern and define the nature of our presence in life. Values are the evidence of the seriousness with which we apprehend and live out our individual existence.

[1] *Pattern and Growth of Personality* (New York: Holt, Rinehart & Winston, 1961), p. 454.

[2] *The Nature of Human Values* (New York: The Free Press, 1973), p. 7.

Unique testimony to the vital importance of values has recently been given by science's renewed attention, even within psychotherapy, to the striking place of values in life. Science has abandoned the effort to be value-free, realizing that even in its most sophisticated measurements in the social sciences, the beliefs and expectations as well as the prejudices of the experimenter may somehow insert themselves. This recognition of value as both a condition for scientific endeavor and a subject for its investigation has led students of psychotherapy, for example, to acknowledge the important role that values play—whether we agree with them or not—in the lives of persons who come for help. One does not quickly try to change, minimize, nor mindlessly trample values upon which other lives have been built. Sensitive scientists are only recognizing what wisdom has known for years: The life that tries to free itself completely of values collapses like an aging star in on itself.

There is even a pragmatic argument made for values, so deep is the person's need for some belief system with which to structure the journey of life. As psychologist Charlotte Buhler has observed, "We are in the dilemma that, while not knowing any longer what to believe in, mankind feels forever compelled to believe in something. Or at least this is true of the vast majority of people at all times."[3] Many observers have noted that when you can believe in anything —when there is no rank of values connected with the things that guide our lives—then you have nothing against which to measure the self, no scale of adequate morality, no goal that makes more sense than any other, no appropriate data to supply the essential foundation for conscience. Stripped of values we are less than human, less than ourselves, and prey to a special anxiety about the meaning of our existence. Expediency—the ultimate in pragmatic solutions—then tells

[3] *Values in Psychotherapy* (New York: The Free Press, 1962), pp. 34–35.

us that what works is what is good, what succeeds is what is acceptable, and what looks good becomes our standard. The recent collapse in America of the pseudomorality based on the careful cultivation of effect rather than substance indicts the ultimate pragmatic view. It is more pragmatic, in other words, to have a value system that has roots, one that matches the needs of the human person rather than one that only seems to work for a short time.

There are many perplexing questions connected with the values through which we live our lives. Values can, for example, be in conflict with each other; two good things can clash head on in what may be one of the most common experiences of our life. Values can be important, but they may in fact never be realized for some people. Self-fulfillment, in other words, may never come to some people because they are caught in situations where this is impossible for no fault of their own and in which they must then make difficult compromises. Many persons do not have an active or penetrating insight into the meaning of their lives. They do not have a broad view of how they all fit together; they move rather from moment to moment, from one situation indeed to another, with hardly time to catch their breath. Many persons have difficulty in understanding and sorting out the values by which they will live because they have been trained carefully to accept the interpretations given to them by others. They are haunted by guilt and fear, by a sense of impending doom and an uneasiness if they are to transgress careful lines set down for them early in life in rather absolute terms. Other people are crippled by internal psychological difficulties that make the realization of their true values extremely difficult for them. The list of complications is almost endless. It is difficult, in short, to speak about values when so many qualifications seem in order.

The problem with values is similar to that connected with sin and guilt, other phenomena closely associated with questions of right and wrong. There are many descriptions and theories, some of them quite effective, along with volumes of analysis, of these events. The problem is that these discussions are frequently so intellectualized that they do not help the average person very much. To say, for example, that a value is that which guides our behavior, or that it is the source of meaning in life to which we commit ourselves, is true in a descriptive sense. The question for the ordinary person, pressed by choices every day, is more urgent. They want to know what they themselves value. The answer to this reflection governs the choice that they will make. It reflects their morality, their sense of right and wrong, and puts the stamp of their own responsibility on their actions. While allowing for the fact that values can develop and can change through education and new experiences, the urgent and almost daily task of discovering in a practical way the values by which we live is essential to any kind of moral life. This is different from accepting someone else's interpretation of our values. It is different even from accepting what, according to Christian or some other teaching, our values ought to be. A sense of ourselves as moral persons emerges when we can face the facts about what our values truly are. What are the guiding principles of our lives? How truly are we committed to them? What would we look like if we could get some over-all picture of them in relationship to our own identity?

The first thing that confronts us in trying to get a better fix on our values is the obstacle of ourselves. We can make it hard for ourselves to understand or to discover things that are important for leading a good or moral life. It is easy, for example, not to think about important things because such weighty subjects sometimes make us uncomfortable or cause us to look away from ourselves in search of distractions. It is easy not to think about what may potentially disturb our adjustment—easy, in other words, to let the

film of our life go undeveloped. It is also easy to fool ourselves about our values and to distort them so that they fit
in with a picture of ourselves that we do not wish to change.
We can always make the world and the circumstances of
our lives do our bidding and fit them into what we want to
hear or what we must believe in order to carry on. This is
not necessarily associated with the truth of ourselves; it is
illogical because it proceeds from the complexities of our
unconscious lives. Some sensitivity, in other words, to our
own capacity for psychological broken-field running is essential as we patiently pursue the task of practically discovering what our real values are. This does not mean that we
should boldly force them out of hiding. It rather suggests
that a journey to self-understanding and to a better-
informed moral judgment about our lives must move at its
own pace and must be governed by an understanding
and acceptance of the way in which as human beings we
can and do behave. We need a basic sympathy for ourselves
in order to find out who we are; we will make it clear to ourselves if, in fact, we give ourselves a chance. We will not
learn, however, if we try to force the answer or subpoena it
in some way out of our unwilling and defensive personalities.

It is not only the force of our unconscious selves that can
make it difficult for us to ascertain our values. We may be
quite conscious of the factors that make us compromise our
values in certain situations, that make us settle for something less than the perfect solution when we are caught in a
dilemma that pits us, for example, between something like
loyalty to our parents and loyalty to our marriage and family
relationships. The conflicts of life are not always between
good and evil; they are frequently between goods of different dimensions, and to see them clearly and to act in ac-
cordance with them is not an easy task. Our values may
also shift with our socioeconomic situation. It is a luxury to

prize the kinds of activities, for example, that can only be carried out in a society whose economic soundness provides leisure than it is in a society where the abject poverty of the people rules out any consideration of art or culture as governing values in everyday activities. It is also probably true that major questions of meaning and value are not consciously thought about by most people. For them it is enough to get through the day.

Yet only we can say what values we really live by. Nobody else can say it for us, and no code, no matter how lofty or true, can by itself get us to respond to its intentions. If we are to discover our values, we must be the ones to find them as they are revealed in our attitudes and behaviors. Only we can see deeply enough into ourselves—if we take the time to do it—to find out what is really going on and why. In the long run, only we can tell what is important to us. The first activity of persons who wish to be serious about right and wrong includes an exploration of their value system. The problem comes to this: How can we approach ourselves with compassion and yet with enough respect and honesty with ourselves to get at the truth? It is easy enough to be a stormy prophet or an obsessive inquirer about our motives—simple, in fact, to upbraid ourselves for fancied guilts or to punish ourselves for psychological reasons. It is far different to examine simply and patiently a picture that emerges of who we are from the activities and responses of any given day of our lives. This process must be done concretely, and it should ordinarily be limited to the context of one day. Once we escape such a simple setting, we can easily theorize about what we are going to do or what we want to do. Our real values, however, emerge from what we do, and our best sense of them can come from examining what we are doing. Some of the questions important in this investigation are as follows:

What are the things that I have the greatest feeling for?

What, in other words, do I make sacrifices for, am I willing to postpone gratification for, or do I plan and dream about? What is the event—or the events—that seem to hold my life together? What do I think or care about when I am not thinking about anything else? What is the background music for my life, the theme that is always there, the music that I am listening to even when I seem to be paying attention to other things?

These questions lead us to some core of our identity that is hard to get at by any other route. Our emotional reactions remain reliable guides to the truth about ourselves. Following these leads back we must deal with their implications about who we are as individual responsible persons. All of these things—when we can consider them carefully—have significance about our attitude toward ourselves, others, the world in which we live, the God who created us, and the ultimate shape of the meaning of our lives. Only as we explore this inner environment of concern can we sense the center of gravity of our own personalities. Through these values we can see reflected the truth of whether we are opened or closed toward other persons, whether we are sealed within our own concerns, or whether we are sensitive to and responsive to the world of other persons around us. There is no fundamental moral viewpoint possible if we cannot see over our own shoulders or if we are always prevented from seeing things from the viewpoint of other persons. The more we can break away from self-absorption the more we move toward a capacity for a more enlightened moral judgment. If we find ourselves locked into self-constructed jails, we may not have reached a point from which we can make any truly moral judgment about anything. We are consumed with self-concern and incapable of moving out or beyond ourselves.

Closely associated questions center on our actual behavior. This puts aside our dreams and our plans, our distant goals, even our vision of what we would like to be. It is concerned with what we actually do with the time and talents that are ours. This is not the same as what we say we do or think that we do. This is one of those areas where fooling ourselves can be raised to a high art. There are fundamental questions with which we must be concerned here. They center on the way we treat ourselves and others. What do I do to myself? Do I have any sense of why I behave this way? What is my characteristic way of dealing with other persons? Am I concerned for their lives, for their separateness, for their becoming more persons in their own right? Do I perceive others as different from me, or do I rather see them as extensions of myself, objects to satisfy emotional needs or agents to be manipulated to the accomplishment of my ends? These may seem hard questions, but they provide a profile that reveals better than anything else the scale of our values.

Such exploration of the self leads us to an appreciation of our typical style. Our style is shaped around our values, and it reflects the goals we are trying to achieve minute by minute and inch by inch every day. It reflects whether we are trying to get closer to people or whether we keep them at a distance, whether we are serious about our work or whether we are trying to get it done as superficially as possible. It reflects our attitude toward the truth better than a lie detector. As we examine our way of dealing with conflicts, we may find more about ourselves than we thought we could. Dealing with difficulties always gives us a good measure of who we are and what we value. Is it important to get them healed and forgotten? Or is our concern with the truth of the matter and with the kind of justice that might be associated with it? What do we do when we discover recurrent problems or difficulties, the whole underside of our personality that has so much unfinished about it? Do we take that seriously or look away from it? As we ask and answer these questions, a pattern emerges, and its main features describe clearly the values that are operational in our lives. These include such basic questions as whether we believe in freedom or control, whether trust and love have any meaning for us, and whether other goals such as pleasure and fairly steady and immediate gratification are more important. The list of these is quite long. One can hardly propose these questions without suggesting to any sensitive person a great many others. The discovery of our values is a never-ending process, but it is absolutely fundamental to achieving a more fully developed and responsible self.

The elements of compassion and patience with the self are important. Perhaps the self-examination should be carried out not so much in the spirit of discovering what we are doing wrong but rather in trying to discover what we are doing right. People seldom ask themselves that question. It is frequently put the other way around: What is it that I am doing wrong? Finding out what is right in our lives builds on the investments we make of our personalities and our talents. What have we bet on in life? Is it persons or things, power or love? Here again, only we can give the answers to these inquiries but, if our objective is to establish greater moral authenticity in our activities, these are the appropriate questions to propose. Closely related are inquiries into whether we let life happen to us or whether we try to take a more active role in shaping its course and giving it meaning. It is hard to be alive at this time in history and not discern a formidable moral implication in the following question: Am I a spectator of the age in which I live, or do I make some contribution, one way or other, to the history of the race?

The examination of what we mean by our religious or spiritual values is also important. Do these remain intellectual, or are they summed up in the careful keeping of obligations, or do we find that we are increasingly committed to a more open-ended, compassionate, and servant role toward others? What, in action, does religion come to in our lives? Is it going to church, putting up with religious services, or do we make room for mystery and for the active experience of religious values in the heart of our existence? Do we enlarge the lives of others, or do we drain life from others? What, in other words, is our practical commitment to the experience of resurrection? Do we ever die to ourselves and our own inclinations for the sake of other persons? Are we related in any way to a dynamic religious experience, or is it a fairly controlled and static entity in our lives? Do we ever give up self-fulfillment for self-transcendence? Or are we so adjusted religiously to a certain pattern of behavior that we are no longer quite sure what religion means in our lives?

It is from practical questions such as these—and many others that a reader might construct—that we begin to sense the hierarchy of our own values. What comes first gives us a point from which we begin to chart a genuine picture of ourselves and to observe the moral outlook that we typically bring to our own lives. One cannot ask these questions without taking life seriously. A person must be alive in order even to wonder about these; the questions are more important than the answers because they awaken us to the truth about ourselves and our lives. And that is the truth that always makes us free.

6

A Sense of Ourselves

What is it like to be a human person? We all think that we have the answer. And so we do, although it is probably never fully or completely stated by any of us even about ourselves. It is a vital question, intimately connected with our expectations about ourselves and about others, a basic question to answer if one is to develop a trustworthy sense of moral judgment. The inquiry represents half the work: Who are we, anyway? And how do we reach some reliable sense of our dignity? What are the steps that enable us to approach ourselves with a seriousness that never becomes stifling solemnity? The question of our identity—of who and what we are—preoccupies people throughout the country. Any book or person who seems to be able to help them forge an answer has a guaranteed audience. People long to get better answers to the fundamentally religious and moral questions about the meaning of their lives. The answers can only be discovered if we begin with a certain tenderness and sympathy for the human race—a feeling this side of both sentimentality and self-pity that helps us to see what is good and hopeful about persons.

In order to begin to answer these questions, we must ask another. Is it necessary always to approach the human person with a moral grid to be pressed down to deliver the kinds of answers moral theologians usually look for? Many theologians who offer us guidelines about life approach the human person solely in terms of right and wrong; they look at the person as good or bad, as a moral success or failure. This is the style of their discipline, the habit of a lifetime as ingrained in their outlook as a feeling for light and shadow is in the artist. But is an evaluation of what is good or bad the appropriate and the only way in which one might approach persons in order to develop some moral sense about them? This presupposition, which derives from the moralist's habitual angle of vision, distorts things right from the start. Is that all there is to see or to know about us? Is it all contained in whether we are good or bad? There may be other ways of approaching men and women without immediately judging them right or wrong, pass or fail, good or bad. We might, for example, try only to understand them.

This seems soft-headed and permissive to many persons who want to get on with the business of declaring things morally correct or incorrect. It seems like some kind of capitulation to the devious human nature that is always trying to squirm out of a definite moral position. It is never, however, an easy thing to be understanding, nor does understanding imply a necessarily permissive stance. To be understanding is far more demanding on the observer than a quick rush to judgment according to traditional moral categories. Understanding demands self-control and a willingness to listen carefully and patiently to what others tell us about themselves. How else can we learn about the human person unless we listen? The meaning of life emerges when we allow persons and things to speak and stand for themselves. Self-deception is easy, as is a claim to certain objectivity while we are subtly reading our own meanings or our own words into our observations. Psychology calls this the Rosenthal effect, after the social scientist who experimentally demonstrated how researchers have a way of finding things they are looking for, of getting the results that they want to get in the first place. Perhaps it is the same for us if we approach human persons with too much confidence in our capacity to judge their moral behavior accurately. Life is richer and more complex than such an outlook presumes, and it demands a sensitivity of moral judgment appropriate to this complexity. This approach does not build on oversimplified black-and-white certainties about the person; rather it looks and listens and, above all, it tries to understand. There is much more to human beings than that which can be captured in a quick *yes* or *no* about their moral behavior.

Take, for example, a woman who comes to tell us about her husband, a man just dead of a terminal illness of which he had knowledge for a few years before the end. Although he kept working and never complained, great strain seeped into his relationship with his wife. He had in the last year and for the first time in his life an affair with another woman. Now, the widow tells us, he is dead, and she is overwhelmed with conflicted feelings about him, their relationship, and the last months of his life. What, she asks, does it all mean, and is it wrong for me to feel the way that I do? What do we say to a person like this? Do we approach this experience with some feeling that we must evaluate it and so place a moral interpretation on it one way or another? Or do we feel that we must evaluate the widow's feelings, branding them as bad or deserved? One can hear the kinds of questions or observations that might be made. "Did he lose his faith?" "Did he give in at the last moment because he had a weak will?" Or perhaps "It's good that you can talk about these things," or "That's terrible," or "You shouldn't feel that way about your dead husband."

It is hard to know how any person could be sure enough about this situation to say any of these things, all of which are based on a self-confident moral judgment that springs from past experience and a willingness to interpret readily the meaning of another's life. This represents an unwillingness to take life, morality, or the other person seriously. Nobody can make any of these judgments with any kind of self-assuredness. Is some decision about the right or wrong of the husband's behavior or the wife's reaction really the important and immediate question? This is not to say that it is an irrelevant question. The wife may be able to answer it for herself if we give her a chance. The important question, however, is whether we understand what it all means. It is not unusual to witness behavior that may be less dramatic but no less symbolic in our own lives or in the lives of those who are closest to us. How do we come to terms with ourselves or with the behavior of others unless we are willing to listen very carefully to the behavior and to penetrate it with the kind of understanding that allows its real meaning to become clear to us?

In the example given, a traditional moralist might be concerned with the nature of the lust and anger that are to some degree involved with it. Another might be concerned about which commandments were broken in the process. If we are sensitive, however, we might first hear and begin to understand the kind of things people do when they are under extreme stress. When a man employs massive defenses against a fatal illness, using denial and enormous self-discipline in order to keep himself going against the pain and to appear normal, he is generally far from that beneath the surface. The price a gravely ill person pays to seem normal on the surface is never small. Does such a massive effort sometimes betray itself? The conflict usually emerges

—as in the example—in symbolic fashion. The individual acts
out the conflicts, seeking release from the pressures that are
self-mounted and that he seems unable to express in any
other fashion. His behavior suddenly changes. He has an
affair, but it has very little to do with lust, fidelity, or any
other commandment. He is acting out sexually something
whose meaning lies deep within him and that he cannot
quite grasp. Through this behavior he is trying to tell himself and those around him something: that he is different,
that his life has changed, that he is fighting against dying,
fighting for his dignity as a man in the only way he seems
able to do. He is putting herculean effort into a solution to
an impossible problem. We would have to listen very carefully in order to catch all the possible significance of this
behavior. The man is saying something, something he cannot quite hear himself, something that others misinterpret,
are confused and hurt by, and to which they find that they
cannot respond. What is the meaning of it? And what is the
morality connected with these last desperate months of the
man's life?

This is like the widower who, lost after his wife dies, suddenly takes to drink, becomes careless about his appearance,
and finds that his children are not only concerned but also
mad at him. "He's different," they say, not realizing how profoundly they are describing this man in a time of loss. He is
different; he is alone, and his sudden turning to alcohol are
efforts to cope with what has happened to him, and lack of
interest in his appearance are symbolic cries about his deso-
lation and his loneliness as well as the signals of his search
for what was so much a part of him before. Is it really
drunkeness? And to what degree in the finer points of moral
judgment? Or is this a man struggling, as persons always do,
waving their hands in a signal to everyone around them
about their distress, saying something we would find touching rather than outrageous if we could really understand

it? Couple to this the blind responses and anger of people who are long oppressed, the terrible kind of violence that sometimes scandalizes or shocks us in people of different color, social class, or country. Do we hear the cries and catch the real meaning? Can the significance of such events ever be separated from the life histories of those who have suffered anguish and frustration for generations? Is it as simple as anger or murder? And who did the murdering, the raging persons seeking their own liberation, or the persons who oppressed them in the first place? It is a symbolic statement, and we all make them almost all of the time.

Truly moral persons listen to everything that they have to say in the many languages besides that of words. We find ourselves and our identity not merely in what we say but also in the total manner in which we express ourselves each day. We are always telling ourselves something; when we are able to read the signals carefully, we understand much more about ourselves and about life in general. We then have a much subtler sense of moral judgment because we are able to see ourselves and others in a far richer perspective. Our problem is that we do not take the messages that we give to ourselves seriously enough. We would be surprised what we would hear if we listened with greater sensitivity. We need a feeling for ourselves, in other words, as total persons who are always trying to reveal rather than conceal things about themselves. It is much like the case of Senator Thomas Eagleton and his celebrated first response, cited the next day by the New York *Times* and boxed as their "quote" for the day, when he was asked to be George McGovern's running mate for Vice President. Senator Eagleton said, in a comment that was accepted as witty but that actually contained a revelation that would only work itself out over the next few weeks, "Senator McGovern called me and asked me if I would run for Vice President. I said *yes, before you change your mind.*" The total Senator

Eagleton was telling the American people something, and telling himself something as well. He was wiser than he seemed to be, more open than he has been judged to be, a man saying as clearly as it could be said, "I cannot help but say yes, but I know that there are things about me that will make you change your mind."

Persons can only be understood in their total psychological presence. One of the first truths about human beings is that, in vocabularies that we may not be able to understand, they are always telling the truth about themselves. It is the same for us. Our chief failing against ourselves may lie in our neglect of what we are so clearly trying to say symbolically about our own truth most of the time. Our failure to love ourselves enough lies in preferring the easy reading, the one that does not go beneath the surface, the one that makes easy moral judgments possible. This can be applied to a wide range of behaviors, both individual and collective. If we could approach with more understanding many of the situations we now hurriedly brand either as moral or immoral on the surface, we would be wiser and far better off. You can apply this, for example, to the difficulties we have had with the problem of pornography in the United States. This phenomenon is easy to condemn but far more difficult to understand. The quick control of the surface manifestations of the problem, as we know from long experience, never entirely eliminates it. It only seems to place it under control, but it does not come to terms with it nor with the basic moral issues that are involved with it. The moral imperative here is to concern ourselves with the general maturity of the country rather than to condemn its immature lustfulness in self-righteous tones.

The difficulties connected with marriage and fidelity require something other than the luxury of condemning people as sinners. People need a chance to be heard in their struggles with their relationships with themselves and each other. People want to move toward the truth about themselves, even though this truth is a very hard one. We make it possible for them to do this through creating a climate of understanding, an attitude that patiently and gently attempts to hear and see everything involved in the lives of people without passing a premature or harsh judgment. The moral truth of our lives only emerges when we can sort ourselves out undefensively in an atmosphere of understanding.

As we understand ourselves and others with this kind of subtlety we begin to see what sin might truly be. It lives in the realm of uncertainty, magic, and superficial interpretation until we can face our living truth in its deepest and most complex dimensions. Anyone who observes human beings over a long period becomes convinced that we live in what can truly be called a sinful condition. It is far from perfect, and it is full of problems; there does seem to be something wrong with all of us. The good life is something we pursue in our struggle to set ourselves right, to get ourselves together, and to join the various aspects of our personalities in an appropriate and healthy relationship to each other. We struggle constantly to harmonize the various layers of our personalities and to heal our conflicts; in the process of doing this, we can feel the mark of original sin in ourselves. Things do not fit together, and life and love do not come easy. Original sin is not merely a theoretical concept; it is the shadow across our pilgrimage. The struggle to be human is the struggle for the wholeness that we understand as holiness. The key to accomplishing this is not staying away from ourselves but getting inside ourselves.

Our concern for morality orients us to decoding our own messages. We cannot achieve a moral sense unless we catch our own communications, because they tell the story of our lives. The *I* that we use to describe ourselves as responsible beings belongs to all of us, not merely to our minds, or just to our feelings, nor to some part of our bodies. What is our style in dealing with ourselves and with others? What are the implications of the way we have learned either to avoid or to deal straightforwardly with our experience? Do we serve ourselves poorly or well by the approach we have to life? Only mature persons who have a feeling for all that they are, can be moral. Morality and maturity are twin objectives, two sides of the goal of human growth to which we are committed by our very breath. Perhaps we are not quite ready to work toward this construct of our total selves as a basis for sensing the richer and more varied tones of our morality. Perhaps we are only at the beginning of realizing what a long journey it will be in order to pass accurate judgments on what we do and how we do it. It is, nonetheless, a good beginning, one that matches the intuitions of contemporary life and the traditional sensitivity of the Gospel. Jesus looked not at surface behavior but at the person beneath. Jesus always looks deeply into people, he knows what is in man, and he does not settle for the superficial and frequently hypocritical style of moral judgment that characterized the Pharisees. As we achieve an understanding of ourselves we possess a more profound sense of morality because we are more in touch with ourselves. We reach a newer and higher stage of integrated and internalized judgments about the meaning of our lives.

It is clear that we are unfinished, that we sin often, and that we are blind to our power to forgive or to change ourselves until we attain a genuine sensitivity to human behavior. Our morality depends on the best use of ourselves and on being able to sense the effects that our use or misuse of our own persons has on those around us. Being moral is the name we give to our effort to overcome the inevitable shortcomings of the human situation. Being less than perfect is not a cause for despair but a condition for growth. The whole Christian life means that we can, with the aid of the Spirit, transcend our imperfect state, go beyond and always become more than we might have expected. We do not accomplish this through our minds, nor through acts of the will; we achieve it when we live and act through our total selves. By presenting ourselves in life just as we are, as whole persons with complex histories and complex modes of expression, we live that way. We plunge into life imperfectly, feeling everything, realizing the cost but still ready to pay it; we never do as well as we would like, but we begin to feel the glorious experience of being fully alive. We become moral presences, subjects rather than objects floating on the tide of existence. In the midst of this we discover evil as a possibility within ourselves rather than as an infection we are liable to catch from the world around us. We discover also that, in a way beyond our imaginings, we become ourselves as we become better acquainted with all that we are. We understand that the basic moral challenge is indeed, against all difficulties and odds, to become our own mystery as truly and richly as we can.

7

A Sense of Responsibility

Our possibilities for good and evil confront us with the question of our personal freedom. Clearly, there is little sense in talking about sin or virtue unless we can in some very real way own our actions, unless what we do stands for us in some way, proclaiming that we are alive and that we make a difference. What an assault of the anonymity of history! A special vision of faith says that the unremembered are not wholly forgotten, and those counted as insignificant lead more than accidental lives. Even unnamed by history, we refuse to be its captives when we can fight our way through the maze to the air of real living and say, "I did this, I possess my own actions, I have not been passive." All the echoing revolutions of our day, both political and theological, pay tribute to our human possibilities for responsibility, for writing our own signatures large and clear on our lives.

Active moral living has never consisted in keeping rules, although this practice does fit our first learning about right and wrong. Something as important as morality cannot be as static as a set of instructions. We live our way into higher morality by maximizing our consciousness of ourselves, not as minds riding bodies bursting with surprising and uncomfortable secrets but as whole persons keyed to an always fuller claim on all that they are. Life never just happens to a genuinely moral person; it is a process, an interaction with existence as wondrous and creative as the birth of a child. It is the continuing birth into life for each of us, the way we lay hold of our identity in and through our love and work. Those who let life happen to them never understand themselves or the continuing rebirth through moral action. They can join with the protesting Orestes who, cut off from his family experience, cried out, "You leave me the liberty of those strands which the winds tear away from a spider's web. They float away in the air. I weigh no more than they, and I'm floating like them in the air."[1] Indeed, persons lacking a sense of identity from within are weightless personalities. To be a moral person requires a living identity in a particular time and place in history. Such persons are in touch with history and with the wellsprings of their own behavior. Acknowledging one's antecedents and the pressures of one's particular external and internal environment while reaching steadily toward one's individuality is the psychological reality of the moral life. It is a complicated business that is destroyed by those who don't give people the freedom to achieve it as well as by those who preach a contemporary and mindless gospel of "fulfillment." That is the main chance of existence, to define our own moral posture; otherwise we never have one at all. A moral stance is our own, or we have missed everything.

Freedom is a goal as much as it is a condition for processing a true sense of ourselves. That is why there is such a growing awareness of the themes of development and liberation in contemporary theology and in papal writings. These

[1] Jean-Paul Sartre, *The Flies* (New York: Alfred A. Knopf, 1947), Act I, Scene 2.

are essential conditions for a truly human and moral life. Most people need freeing from the oppression of prejudice, ignorance, or political domination, as well as from the peril of their own great and small fears. People need both room and encouragement—profound demands of any religious vision—to sense their humanity and to know the mystery rather than just the misery of existence. An enlightened concern for freeing persons to attain an adult sense of themselves—and a little progress is a lot of progress here—is the proper object of both Church and state.

The moral concern of Churches is pre-eminently to point out and fight for the conditions of life in which human beings can truly become acquainted with themselves so that they can both taste and feel the experience of their own freedom, so that they can know that they are alive. This is why there is a perennial battle to make institutions renew themselves so that they can perceive and deal with people as persons; that is a prime moral function of institutions, but one dangerously easy to forget. Freedom to become moral is not a luxury; indeed, a classic Pauline theme contrasts freedom and law. To be free—interiorly free—is the goal. The law, symbolic of oppressive forces, is a weight because its controlling power can inhibit the discovery and real experience of the self. Laws are not bad; they are just not everything and can never supply the complete source or measure of morality.

This theme may be discovered in many places other than in St. Paul; it is an abiding concern of history and pervades the literature and myths of the ages. The person is always charged with realizing and accepting his or her own individuality. This eternal journey toward the truth about ourselves contains the elements of the essential Christian pilgrimage. It is not a trip to be made in an unknowing or distracted state, nor is it one that can be completed by following the directions of some outsider. It is a journey each of us is invited to make and that we must make for ourselves. The important business of being an individual is connected with attaining the responsibility that goes with a free sense of the self. Morality is not just connected with avoiding evil at all costs; it is also connected with coming to terms with all that life contains without pulling back or defensively avoiding it. Nobody has an easy task in carving out a free-standing self.

We have become aware of some of the many forces with which we must deal as we struggle to achieve our individuality. There is, for example, our genetic inheritance, which determines so much about who and what we can become. Add to this the question of our environment, both physical and psychological, as a strong shaper of our attitudes, interests, and general self-regard. The environment houses the powerful forces of religious and ethnic traditions, family prides and prejudices, as well as a hundred other factors that have strong impacts on the developing self. Many of these influences travel with us in our unconscious life, emerging only in our defenses or our neurotic styles of handling things. We may have a limited awareness of how we live out our unconscious scenarios, or of the ways we hide and reveal ourselves at the same time. They are too much a part of our unverbalized self for us to be able to notice them very clearly. Out of this mix we are invited to shape a sense of ourselves, of our limitations and our abilities, enough at least to be able to proclaim a responsible "I am" in the face of life.

The worst of all curses against persons lies in denying them the opportunity to take up this difficult task. Sometimes our motives in doing this seem to be good. We want to shield others from life so that they will not be hurt by it or to help them avoid the places where we know that sorrow lurks. Deny this chance at finding themselves to people and they will moan as Orestes did. They will feel that they have

no content as persons, no gritty substratum that even if un-
predictable is still very real. Protected persons spend their
existence trying to meet the expectations of others because
they have no personal account to draw on, no sense of their
own lineage nor of their individual meaning. Denying people a chance to discover themselves, even when this may be
very painful, disinherits them and prevents them from ever
attaining a true moral sense. And it is all done in the name
of good. That is why do-gooders are such a perennial danger
and why paternalism is such a profound scourge to persons.
In the name of saving people's lives, these attitudes and the
actions they motivate actually take people's lives away.

What such forces work on us under their benign flags of
battle takes away basic life experiences from us. It never
helps to make us look away from ourselves. In processing
everything that is a part of ourselves, acknowledging the
harvest of complex influences and understanding always a
little better the reasons for our reactions, we come to know
and be our true selves. This relationship to all that we are,
long neglected in many lives, is the basis for our free moral
activity. But people can get through life without ever confronting anything but a small portion of their own reality.
They miss life, its glorious risks and its highest moments of
self-definition, the choices that can be our own, accepting
and dealing with our identity with an increasing responsibility for who constitutes the essence of our personal moral
growth.

This close-up focus on the self only seems related to selfishness. An achieved openness to our real experience, however, denies us the narcissistic luxury of illusions about
ourselves. It forces us to live in the real world rather than in
a defended one where we keep at a distance both from ourselves and from others. The entrapped ego is rescued only
through the awareness that opens it gently to the world of
persons and events around it. As we break through the con-

fines of self-absorption, we enter the world of other persons and begin to express ourselves with a new and heightened regard for them. This enriching liberation is never accomplished alone but always in relationship to others. Psychological threads lead back to our parents, our relatives, our peers, our teachers, and our friends. It is most significantly underscored in our relationships of love.

What other moral aim could Churches have but to work to achieve these conditions and try to insure a chance for everybody for a free and human life? What else could be better for them to do? The Churches, through their preaching, liturgy, and sacramental life, powerfully emphasize and celebrate the events and relationships through which we achieve a sense of our moral selfhood. The sacramental system is not magical, nor does it point only to another world of reality beyond this; it is far more fundamental and humanizing, far closer to life than many people have supposed. The sacramental Church can point to those moments of self-discovery and expansion in which we begin to sense our own meaning and grasp something of the essence of life. Some Churches have demanded moral behavior far more than they have fought for the conditions in which to achieve it. Preaching about morality by itself is an incomplete pastoral response unless Churches actively help people enter into their own lives as wholeheartedly as possible. Moralizing keeps people at the edge of life; a truly moral Church helps people find their way through it.

What does being responsible involve? Pivoting on expanding self-understanding, it confronts us with the hard work of determining the values by which we live and the direction in which we are going to move. It is surprisingly easy to go through life without thinking much about these things. It is simple to take for granted the values presented by a particular culture and not to examine these in much depth. Only later may we discover that these deliver neither meaning nor deep satisfaction; we find, in fact, that we are left without choices because all the supporting beams of our culture have snapped at once. Survival may then become more important than anything else, and the freedom to move with some enjoyment and some savor of life becomes more remote all the time. This has happened more than once to people who never thought for themselves; they become the trapped passengers outward bound, the stranded pilgrims on a lost horizon.

Being responsible means taking the time to decide the nature of the good moral life. It involves us in integrating our religious beliefs with the style of our existence, and that only sounds easy. Taking on responsibility helps us learn that love is not a solution but a complex challenge and that life consists in making investments rather than in cashing them in. Lots of people say that love is the highest value in their lives, but many have little grasp of what it means or what it asks of them. A surprising number of people are hesitant to ask whether the love in their lives is real or not. How can they possibly invoke a law of love to sharpen their moral sensitivity if they have only a partial or distorted understanding of its meaning? How can people judge what is right or wrong if they have not thought deeply about what is important to them, what they count as worth having, and what they feel to be lasting values? The way to responsibility is difficult and is filled with hard questions and sharp turns; obviously there is no secret formula for finding your way with it. There is just working it out every day in terms of convictions we make our own, in being able to write our own name on our presence in life—the signal that says "I am here"—because we take ourselves quite seriously as human beings.

This responsible awareness of the self opens us to many levels of our existence—to some, in fact, to which we may previously have paid little heed. The average person, for example, may not listen to the soundings of the unconscious nor to the messages of his dreams. These are not meaningless or random events, however; they are us, and the more we can open ourselves to the layers of our existence, the more we sense and respect our own personhood. Our dreams are not mass-produced in Hollywood and distributed to the theater of our minds. They are one of our potent ways of talking to ourselves.

The Spirit of truth is operative whenever we make a genuine effort to look closely and sensitively at our own personalities. We can count on the Spirit to guide us to the truth whenever we attempt to be honest, when we try to hear what we are saying to ourselves and to take sufficient account of it to integrate it into our presence in life. This is a powerful way of respecting ourselves, of neither burying nor squandering our talents; it takes us in a direction different from that of self-defeat. To grow in command of oneself through listening, investigating, and searching out everything that takes place inside of ourselves is, in itself, a profoundly moral activity. This does not work only for the analyst's couch; it is the work of life itself. Through it we derive an active share in the mystery of revelation, the dazzling and exciting experience of our own inner world that occurs whenever we take the time to listen with understanding to our own experience.

That this is not a solitary expedition is also part of the mystery. We are never alone in discovering ourselves. Whenever we truly touch the lives of others we find out something about ourselves. This mystery of meeting another and entering more deeply into life because of our relationship with the other is one of life's central experiences. It alerts us more to our own meaning, breaking our shell of narcissism wide open, and enables us to experience others in a way that is impossible when we are totally self-contained. This transaction lies at the heart of life, the mystery of how we are changed by drawing close to and learning how to love other persons.

Such processes are never totally rational. Completely rational experiences of growth match neither our needs nor our nature. This is part of what we discover in our efforts to take more responsibility for our own identity. We have to let ourselves go in life, take the risks—let ourselves die—in order to find ourselves in greater fullness. We accomplish this with the raw material of our genuine selves; it doesn't work with a façade or with pretense. In honesty to another alone are we changed.

Morality is the product of our surrender to truly human experiences, to letting ourselves penetrate, possess, and share the levels of nonrational and unconscious communication that are part of our identity. As we actively surrender to these moments, the Spirit assists us, and we emerge with a deepened sense of our own identity and a better appreciation of the identity of others. This is a reciprocal experience rooted in the continuing dynamic of revelation. We never learn just about ourselves; that is narcissistic fascination. We begin to feel our moral personalities when we sense ourselves in relationship to the others who make a difference to us and to whom we make a difference. This moral intuition about the effects of our actions and attitudes on other persons is fundamental to any heightened responsibility for our lives. This primary moral awareness arises, even in its primitive stages, in a social context and reaches its highest refinement in our relationships of friendship and love. When we enter these with some sense of self-possession we are free to travel much more deeply into self-understanding because we see now also with the eyes of someone with whom we share love.

This provides a new perspective because we are forced by such relationships to develop a more acute moral awareness; now we are responsible to somebody else. This demands a subtler moral judgment than the idea of being responsible for somebody else. Responsibility goes beyond carrying out a duty or exercising paternal protectiveness. In being responsible to each other, persons feel the challenge of mature moral behavior that is based on what they can do, for good or for ill, to each other. It draws the moral equation for us in existential terms. What I do makes a difference to someone else; what I feel, what I believe—even when these are not revealed to the other—have an effect for which I am responsible. We leave marks on each other all the time, traces of our moral presence. This is my doing, and I can read what I do in the lives of those around me.

What are the signs of having achieved a sense of our own moral and personal identity? What are the guidelines we might use to judge whether we are responding to life in an authentically moral way? The first of these is a sense that we are acting with our total personalities. When we use *I*, it incorporates all the levels of our being of which we can in some way be aware. The *I* is, in a sense, an integrating statement under which we stand in our full responsible identity. In other words, morality does not concern just our thoughts or our feelings. Nor can it be associated merely with our external behavior and still deserve the term human. We cannot, for example, successfully separate our sexuality from our personality without doing damage to our moral sense through destroying the integrity of our own persons. *I* do things. *I* am a subject rather than an object, and the more keenly I achieve my own sense of identity the more deeply I experience life and the more responsible I am as a human being. We marshal the forces of ourselves, making ourselves present in the truth of our own existence, when we live in contact with our full selves, when we stand on the moral bridge of our lives in our own name.

This is a fundamental way of loving ourselves enough, of paying enough attention to ourselves so that we govern

rather than are governed. Only through this attitude can
we work through the emotional snarls that obstruct and interfere with our sense of responsibility. As subjects—as *I's*
—we take a stand that belongs really to us. We are not likely
to do any of these things perfectly. Being a person is more
of a process than an event. We are, indeed, always becoming, growing in wholeness as we live in honesty. Such an
attitude not only establishes our responsibility but also enables us to deal with guilt in a manner that is both sensitive
and sensible. It enables us, in other words, to avoid unnecessary neurotic guilt and to see our moral selves in cleaner
and clearer focus.

A second feature of self-possession is that we do not view
others through the cloud of our own narcissistic self-concern.
We see other people as subjects rather than as objects. Because we possess a sense of our own existence, we appreciate what it means for others to be persons, to have
lives in their own right that are separate from ours and toward which we must exhibit respect and concern. Others are
not just for our use or for our manipulation, not just for our
entertainment or pleasure. Even the ones we love most have
a claim on a life that is their own; nobody can live morally
just for someone else, nobody can throw his own separateness away. Love dies in the lives of people who blur their
vision of each other as persons; our moral sense awakens us
precisely to an active appreciation of the presence of others
in life. We take other persons seriously because we understand something of what it means to take ourselves seriously. This is where sensitivity, the sacrifice or curtailment
of our own rights—the whole process of the healthy compromise of living—makes demands on us.

Here, perhaps more than in any other moral transaction,
we are challenged by the gospel imperative to die to ourselves. This never-ending process continually refines our
moral sensibility by forcing us to examine our tendency to

view everything in terms of our own needs. Through it we become aware of the effects we have on others, and these cannot be denied, brushed aside, or ignored as though they did not exist. In what we think and how we react to others we define our fundamental morality. We may ask, therefore, whether there can ever be anything that is casual between two persons. This can only occur when persons perceive each other as objects rather than as subjects. It is clearly possible to have sex without love, but only if we view others as objects. How difficult it would be to use others only for sexual gratification if we could perceive them as subjects, breathing, feeling persons with a right not to be used or manipulated by others. The highest realm of adult morality is invisible, a world that exists around and between persons, a world where measurements fail because they cannot chart the powerful exchanges that take place there. We are most real in what we do with our total personalities to each other.

The concerned person must ask questions about the self constantly, not in an obsessive concern about perfection, but in a healthy search for what, in any complicated situation, defines our moral position. We look for what speaks for ourselves most fully. If we do not ask these difficult questions, we reject our responsibilities, perhaps not with complete deliberation, but with a certain disrespect for our moral possibilities. We exile ourselves from a fuller life and fail to construct that court in which we are charged to confront ourselves about the nature of our choices. We are moral in proportion to the amount of ourselves we make present in our decisions and actions.

How far have we journeyed toward a deepened sense of ourselves and our responsibilities? It is not that we need fundamental moral examples sketched out again. We have, if we are honest, heard them many times. The difficulty is not that we have not been told; it lies in incorporating what we know about right and wrong into our own lives as culture shifts and conditions change. Right and wrong have not disappeared. Responsibility for judging them—for fleshing out our own decisions about good and evil in our own lives—has come now to us, and we are unfamiliar with it. Sin is always easy to see when somebody else points it out. We only get a good look at it, however, when we look at it closely for ourselves—when we get close enough to ourselves as persons to see what, despite the complexities of our lives, we can do to ourselves and others, when we can glimpse with some freedom a vision of our own responsibility for the moral shape of our lives. We do not need to be told again; we need to take ourselves seriously enough to work through to our own moral stance in life.

The phrase "being our own person" has been demeaned in our culture. It has been associated with a million insignificant manipulations of our egos—with what we smoke or drink—so that we can perceive ourselves as independent and well defined when we do not even understand the challenges of having a separate identity. Being responsible means the end of an easy, self-centered existence—but it also means the end of an empty life. It means reclaiming ourselves and seeing life and other persons anew, of taking risks and getting hurt, of loving and being loved, of tasting loss and knowing joy—but also of knowing what it means to be alive. Morality is a very serious but not a solemn business.

8

Living

If morality cannot be summed up in individual actions, how can it be understood? We are moral in the slant and style of the personal existence through which we hold all the actions of our lives together. This is the substantial material of the self, the personal essence that gives form and direction to our activity, the ego of our freedom and responsibility. We are moral just as we are loving or religious, not now and then or only in matters of some grave moment, but as we live through every day. We have to fly each day down to a landing the way a pilot becomes one with his balking plane as he coaxes it to earth in stormy weather. Good or bad are in the balance all the time, the good or bad generated, encouraged, or performed by us. What do we do all day? We live out our moral lives, whether we recognize this fact or not.

Morality is not a sometimes thing. The only way a dynamic morality, one that allows people to take themselves seriously, exists, is in and through the way we live with each other. We are, in other words, always working through our moral positions, constantly revealing ourselves and defining ourselves in our love and our work. What we do in larger moments—perhaps in temptations to lie, cheat, or fail others —is all of a piece with the person we are all day long every day. How, in fact, does this work out, and how can persons become more aware of the moral face of their everyday existence? Obviously we are always coming to terms with ourselves and, in this life, we never finish the process. That is why we never lay hold of a completely finished moral position. Nor is morality anything, as we have noted, that we ever do just by ourselves. There is a continuing fallacy about the possibility of the isolated existence, the believer as rugged individual standing alone between conscience and God to render an account of life. The notion that we are romantic exiles going it alone must be put aside if we are to understand operational morality. We are, like it or not, hooked up with each other, and it is as we live through our multiple relationships with integrity that we carve out an enduring moral stance. We are implicated in network morality because we never act alone and because the idea of living at a distance from people in moral purity alone with God is, except in a very few instances, an insupportable and highly questionable escape from life. We are connected in the human condition, and what we do and how we respond to the crises that constantly fall across our lives in an authentic application of the domino theory make clear the intimate connection between our moral behavior and our sense of being in relationship to others.

Even though the stage is sometimes set that way in our imagination, we never really do anything just to ourselves, not even in a last lonely act of self-destruction. Just as suicide is filled with implications for other persons, so we constantly send and receive messages about what we mean or where we stand in relationship to one another. That is where the essence of morality lies, in the actual living of life with each other. The shape of our moral presence is therefore determined by our awareness of how our shadows fall always across each other's paths. Being moral or immoral is defined in and through our style of personal presence—in the posture we assume—and the room we take up or cede to others in living together. Morality's fibers spark, then glow, and finally burn brightly in the social reality of standing in life with each other.

This is admittedly no easy task; it takes us a long time to grasp its essence, and we may do this only intermittently, getting a clearer vision as we catch sight of our true selves. We live at a fairly low level of consciousness until we get our grip on our own identity and draw more purposefully close to others. It is not surprising at the earlier stages of our personal development that we need the rules and regulations that come from family, friends, and the institutions of our culture. Socialization is a complex process, and there is no way of making things easier or of permanently shortening processes that depend on and are mediated through time itself. The important things about us are all tied up with each other, the mystery of time, and the startling complexity of growing up. To participate in the socialization of human beings is a highly moral task, which involves more than getting the young to behave the way we would like them. Our morals are learned to some great extent; we are, therefore, the teachers of morality to succeeding generations. It is one of the processes through which we reveal our own moral position quite clearly. What we have is what we hand on, howsoever poorly or well developed it may be. This occurs through the social process; sometimes we can see the invisible aspects of our moral behavior better in teaching the young than in our other relationships. We may be more aware of the killing effects of deception, for example. We know that if we tell a child one thing when we really mean something else, the mixed message gets through. We confuse or bewilder children when we raise ambiguous symbols before them. We know that we cannot merely pretend to like children if something inside of us betrays the truth of our feelings. The real message comes directly from our insides to theirs, bypassing the intellect, to which we sometimes give such exclusive authority and power in matters moral.

Persons affect each other in many ways, however, and, although we are ready to believe that we can corrupt the young by hypocrisy, we forget that we continue to corrupt each other by similar failures. Dynamic morality reminds us that, whatever the context, we define the rightness or wrongness of our actions through our total personalities. Our thoughts and actions come together in our persons, and we are moral in our specific identities or we are incapable of any meaningful morality at all. Morality is something we accomplish, in other words, with all of ourselves, and the modes of its expression and transmission are the wavelengths of our interpersonal lives.

We are moral, for example, when we are trying to make room for another person in our lives, and when, in order to accomplish this, we attempt to overcome the mass of prejudices, distractions, or indolent self-interest that keeps them locked outside of us. There is a profound positive morality in listening to another with as much of ourselves as possible. This is a way of receiving others and of giving them the gift of our own presence at the same time. It not only re-creates the basic religious experience of dying to ourselves in order to share life with others, but it also does, in fact, change both us and others. We are resurrected by such a process. It is a basic human exchange of extraordinary seriousness. That is why it is also a serious sin to reject others, not to listen to them, or to relate to them in terms of prejudiced perceptions of them. These are choices we can easily make and often do make in order to save our own world just for ourselves.

That is the choice not to be a subject in life and not to receive others as subjects into our life space. Perhaps one of the best rules of thumb we possess about our moral selves comes to this: Am I acting like a subject in life, and am I treating others as subjects? Or do I treat myself and others as objects instead? It is not hard to tell the difference between these attitudes and discerning them accurately is a highly moral activity. It is helpful, in this regard, to recall that art is highly moral precisely insofar as it senses and responds to human beings as subjects; it is an evocation of what it means to be a subject in life. The same deadness that is bred by art that treats human beings as objects is what we generate when we treat persons the same way.

Becoming a self is at the very center of the moral reality of living. There are several important aspects of achieving the complex and unique self-awareness of our personalities. We become subjects, in other words, through an increased consciousness of everything that is true of us. Only subjects are capable of moral decisions and of affecting the moral growth of other people. It is only as subjects that we achieve and express any measure of freedom, take on any responsibility for our lives, and reject the passivity that fatally paralyzes our moral possibilities.

Morality demands that we perceive ourselves as agents in life. This implies a sense of being connected with our activities, of owning what we do, and of recognizing these as evidence of our intentions and our identity. Many people are unfortunately uncomfortable with the idea of being an agent self in life. Sometimes this difficulty arises because they have never been helped sufficiently to develop a satisfactory sense of themselves. This happens, for example, when, in critical stages of life, young persons are force-fed the guilty appraisals of adults about their actions that do not merit these feelings. It is common for people to feel a lack of self-confidence—and therefore to be inhibited in

possessing their own actions—when they have not been
prized or made to feel worthwhile in the eyes of those who
are influential during their period of growing up. It is very
difficult for people who are crippled in this way to develop
an accurate moral sense. They constantly confuse their own
lack of self-confidence and their own neurotic guilt for a
more accurate rendering of their life experiences.

Persons who are assisted in understanding their own
inner experience and who are reasonably loved and sup-
ported by surrounding adults are capable of a much clearer
view of themselves. They feel at one with themselves and so
can feel a proper source of accomplishment at performing
what is right in life as well as a fitting sense of guilt as a result
of failures. The self as agent—cleared of neurotic interfer-
ence—is an essential aspect of a personal moral presence in
life. On this hinges any perception of oneself as being able to
act positively and influentially in shaping or pursuing one's
goals or destiny. A sense of ourselves as capable of decision
and choice is intimately related to a sense of moral power.

Closely allied is an understanding of the self as continuous, as in possession of a perduring identity that gives some
consistency to our lives. Things do not happen out of the
blue. We are not suddenly different people overnight. The
blueprints are always there in advance, and only persons
who learn to read these can possess a comfortable picture
of themselves moving through time in a steady moral fashion. When one's view of the self is disjointed or distorted,
it is very difficult to develop this awareness of being an
individual person passing through the experience of life in
time. The stability of the self in relationship depends to a
large extent on our established sense of identity and our
understanding of ourselves as having a core of selfhood that
abides despite a multitude of external changes. It is true
that some persons are surprised—in middle age, for example
—to discover new facets of their personalities. One may

suddenly declare, "I'm not the same person I was when I got married," or something similar to that. What such persons are really saying is that they are suddenly becoming aware of aspects of themselves to which they had not previously adverted. Their subjective surprise may be genuine; the absolute newness of any aspect of their personality is, however, questionable. Self-discovery and the final emergence from the wreckage of one's adolescence—these can happen far later in life than they are scheduled to occur. When this is the case there is a discontinuity in the person's moral sense of judgment and in the person's understanding of what it means to be in relationship with others.

Most of our active life is lived with some sense of being in relationship to other persons. It is the heart of moral living, as we have suggested, and it is in exploring and identifying the way we make ourselves present to others that we find the particular character of our own moral development. Without a sense of self, one cannot be in anything that could be termed a relationship with another person. There are a great many people who are precisely in this situation. They want closeness and intimacy but, lacking any real sense of themselves, they are incapable of being the subject of any deep relationship at all. They feel this lack, but they do not have sufficient possession of their own identity to enable them to love, or, for that matter, to be loved. Moral living is a confusing enterprise for them.

A psychological and moral self is also perceived as a locus of values, goals, and ideals. These are powerful sources of inspiration and example in shaping the moral actions of each one of us. In the morally sensible person the picture of the self fairly accurately represents what the self truly is. When these two pictures fit together there is also a goal that matches the realistic possibilities of this well-identified moral subject. Moral and life ideals are likewise perceived in relationship to a well-defined sense of self. In other words, the person with a realistic appreciation of the self also chooses ideals that are within the grasp of that self; they are the attainable, workable hypotheses for their moral human living. Only when people have a distorted or uninformed sense of themselves do they hold up ideals that they cannot reach and then make demands on themselves that they can never satisfy. They are always falling short and harvesting undeserved and crippling guilt. People who lack a basic sense of themselves tend to distort everything else in relationship to this perspective. It is impossible to lead a moral life if one's ideals are far beyond one's capacity to attain them. This is not to say that people should settle for anything resembling cynicism; it is to observe how easily a wide gulf of amorality develops when people mouth ideals from which they are, in fact, permanently estranged. This may be the particular fate of politicians, preachers, or others who have public positions from which to point to and uphold moral ideals. There is nothing worse for the morality of the people, however, than an ideal that does not match the possibilities of the human condition. Such ideals have occurred often enough in the history of the world. They include perfectionism, radical hedonism, and a wide variety of intermediate and inappropriate visions. Morality lies in helping people be what they can be; it is immoral to try to make them into something they cannot be.

What does one ask about being a self in, for example, the simple example of friendship? What does it mean in a moral sense to be a friend? It begins, of course, with taking ourselves seriously enough to accept the reality of friendship and the responsibilities involving another person that are intimately associated with it. An obsessive person might well drive himself crazy trying to define the parameters of his friendships. Healthy people, unmarred by restrictive guilt, can ask and answer these questions without experiencing undue stress. This is not to say that they must propose these inquiries on every occasion in which they enter into friendship. That is not necessary in a mature moral life. People move forward quite unself-consciously when they believe in and live by humanly relevant moral principles.

There are serious questions to ask about being a friend, because friendship has a profound meaning in any moral or religious scheme of life. Far from being a matter of indifference, as some unfortunate interpretations of the gospel made it seem in recent centuries, friendship is a testing ground for and a manifestation of our moral selves. A person can ask, then: What does it mean to be with this person at this time and in this place? Do I perceive the other as a whole person, or am I interested only in some aspect or part of the person that affords pleasure or is of some interest to me? Do I see this other as a separate person with a life, rights, and goals of his or her own? Or is the other perceived rather as some extension of my own self, something I can use or manipulate as I please, something for my satisfaction more than for anything else? Am I myself with this other person, or am I presenting something that is essentially false or distorted? Is my response to this person for the sake of the person or for the sake of what this person may be able to do for me?

I wonder, a person might ask, what this relationship does mean? Do I look beyond its boundaries, or am I ready to settle, in this instance, for calling something friendship that is not strong enough to be friendship at all? Am I willing to be sexually interested in this person on a limited basis, cutting off all other possibilities or implications? And what does that say about my moral presence in this situation?

It may be difficult to propose, but it is basic to explore the question of whether we believe that we make any difference in what we do or how we act in relationship to others. It is possible that, unconsciously at least, we feel that our own ease or needs justify any manipulation or use of the other

that we see fit. We may make a case for releasing control of
our impulses, if only in fantasy, in order to use this person
for ourselves. It is appropriate to wonder whether we have
learned to respect people or whether we completely blot
out all the implications of this word, preferring to gaze only
at a very restricted vision of this particular relationship without asking any questions that might embarrass or cause us
to search ourselves and our moral stance more fully. If we
are serious about life, we realize that whenever we draw
close to others we do something to them, just as they, in
turn, always do something to us. Can this ever be without
moral shape or meaning? It is possible, after all, to poison
the space between us and others by unspoken and un-
admitted deceits, half truths, efforts to impress or distract
or just to make ourselves feel good. It is possible, for a wide
variety of reasons, to exaggerate or distort what I know to
be the truth in order to keep someone under my influence.
Is there a slow killing both of ourselves and of others in the
accumulation of these small but telling defects? Do we think
that we have escaped the meaning of morality because nobody else knows about this but us? Is there ever a time when
"no one else is hurt"?

In the long run, the question comes down to the quality
of our presence in relationship to others in life. To what
degree am I present, and to what purpose? As we pursue
inquiries like this, some of us may discover that we seldom
live outside of ourselves or in response to anything but our
own needs. It may look differently to others, and we may be
applauded by the world, given citations, and gladly accept
any and all acclamation. Yet a closer view might show that
to achieve notoriety is the chief motivating engine of our
existence and that we look at others mostly as means to
guarantee that we accomplish this. If, in fact, we discover
that we are still locked within ourselves, then we are pos-

sessed by our narcissism and are still far from living a moral life.

Closely related to this can be our interest in or our willingness to try to change ourselves or to grow into a more developed moral and personal presence in life. There are moral implications connected with our willingness to listen and to try to understand our own inner experience rather than to force on ourselves some interpretation from outside that may mislead us and provide a false sense of direction for our moral strivings. It is possible for people to stay at a fairly superficial level in life without much awareness of themselves and without ever pulling together the moral posture that brings them to life and enables them to experience the meaning of their own existence.

That is why some sins are called deadly. They prevent us from experiencing life, and they also interfere with our capacity to give or expand the lives of those around us. While we have reflected on only a few aspects of the questions that help us to discover and reveal our true moral selves, these do indicate the seriousness with which our own identity and presence as persons must be taken. It is also possible that if we do not take ourselves seriously, we will miss the chance not only to be moral but also to penetrate life deeply enough to understand and celebrate our own existence. We may be born and be buried and never understand the time between these events.

9

Sinning

What happens when we sin? This inquiry has largely been answered with descriptions, theological in nature, of what must take place to justify the Christian interpretation of sin as such a perennial and horrifying constant of history. Without sin, the Churches teach us, the redemptive work of Jesus Christ would lack meaning. Central to the Christian understanding of history is the conviction that we are sinful people and that salvation, as God's gift through Jesus, frees us from sin's coils. One can accept all this and still not come any closer to understanding what occurs inside of us when we commit a sin. How do we do it, in other words, and why should sin be so difficult to define if it is indeed so much a part of our human condition?

We have passed from a teaching tradition that emphasized external actions as identifiable as sin to a new era in which theologians have tried to combine this former view with the insights of the new learning about the person that has taken place over the past century. Sin has, therefore, been internalized and is now more frequently described in terms of our failure to love, and, in particular, in our failure to love our neighbor. Anyone who has ever taken sin seriously already knew that it could never consist merely in things outside of us, and that something so powerful in its implications and its effects could only exist as a product of our own inner selves. But, in the metaphors of sin, what was once a something outside ourselves has become a nothing inside ourselves.

Most of our definitions and descriptions of sin have not been fully satisfactory; they have been drawn up largely to meet the needs of explaining how such human calamities could occur in the face of a loving God. Such efforts to interpret sin largely meet what are conceived to be God's needs for an adequate description of what it could mean for his creatures to turn aside from the path of salvation that he has opened freely to them. The imagery is not without merit. It gives us a feeling for a strange power, somewhat hazily described, through which we can, in fact, separate ourselves from God himself. But the problem still remains: If this phenomenon is so pervasive and so powerful, why cannot we describe it more clearly to ourselves? Why have we depended on authorities outside of us to categorize and to point out our sins? Why do we search even now for modernized directions from outside to help us understand what we can only fashion from within? If this power belongs to us, how else can we understand it except through searching deeply for its secrets in our own experience?

If sin is a personal human event, then we should be able to describe how it feels to commit one. We should also have some fair sense of what happens to us when we are the authors of sin in our lives. We may be bewildered about sin at the present time because it is so difficult to re-establish a link of responsibility with ourselves in regard to sin. For one thing, since sin was considered for so long to be something external, we may miss the convenience and functionality of such a way of perceiving it. It is also difficult, given the insights and progress of psychology and anthropology, to sort out what is impelled from what is willed, what rises from the shadows of the unconscious and what proceeds freely from our own choices in our own behavior. We are inheritors, it would seem, of much that has gone before us, and we are also shaped strongly by the learning that takes place, especially in the early stages in our lives. How can we reach through to a sense of and command of self that could approximate the kind of self-possession that would obviously be required to commit something powerful enough to cut us off from God's good pleasure?

Committing sin is not a childish game. It requires a relative maturity, a sense of knowing what we are doing, and an adequate internalization of our moral principles and beliefs. We also need some appreciation of ourselves as agents who can act with some degree of freedom in making choices in life. Nor is any idea of sin possible if we lack a sense of reciprocity in our relationships with other persons; in other words, unless we can sense the effect of our actions or our omissions—or even our thoughts—on other persons, we may have only a remote idea of sin as a concrete reality in our lives.

The first principle that we can accept is that it takes maturity to be able to sin. This is not to deny that sinlike events or pseudosinfulness will be reflected in our behavior in many ways. But sinfulness that proceeds from psychological immaturity is hardly strong or well shaped enough to deserve the name of sin. The appearance of sin, no matter how it has been described in history, is a necessary intellectual category—material sin, it has been called—but it does not help when we confuse it with the actions that can be labeled as genuinely sinful. It is not wise, then, to equate sin with immaturity, although some authors have come to do this in recent years. Unless we can be held responsible for our own immaturity—a doubtful proposition at best—then immaturity may sound like a contemporary interpretation of sin but, because it places sin beyond our adult control, it simply does not serve. Immaturity is not sturdy enough to be the source of real sin. There are adult moments in which we may choose to be immature that might qualify as sinful, but the fact that we are voyagers—always growing and never finished—is not something about which we have much choice. If immaturity is a sin, then being human is a hopelessly sinful enterprise. We may regret some of the foolish things, the things called the sins of our youth, but they do not belong enough to the realm of conscious choice to deserve the label of serious sin.

Neither can we call our psychological defenses sin. Defenses are fundamentally unconscious, and so they are also outside the possibility of free choice. It may be unattractive to be defensive, and defenses may lead to what could be described as reprehensible acts, but these common psychological mechanisms are not in themselves sinful. Defenses do indeed deceive, as, for example, when we rationalize by giving a good reason but not the real reason for our actions. Deception is one of the chief functions of psychological defenses. Only as we mature and get some insight into the way we can fool ourselves and attempt to fool others does the possibility of actively and consciously choosing deception become a possible and potent one for us.

The liabilities connected with growing up in adverse psychological circumstances are well known. There may indeed be more truth than we sometimes admit in the fact that people are generally more sinned against than sinning. The handicaps, psychological and otherwise, they acquire in their earliest years do indeed work against their developing a true consciousness of the meaning of or capacity to commit a serious sin. Being sinned against makes it difficult for individuals to complete their human development as adults who are capable of explicit good or evil. Growing is a hazardous and long-term business, and we confuse the matter of identifying sin when we associate it too much with the conditions of achieving our maturity. It may take a long time to learn how to sin; we only have glints or partial intuitions about it until we understand our own power, that two-edged force that enables us both to love and also to hurt in life. This is hardly a novel idea; the traditional conditions that the Roman Catholic Church set down for committing serious sins—grave matter, sufficient reflection, and full consent of the will—merely describe the hard-bought characteristics of adult choice. You have to know who you are and what you are doing in order to commit sin.

The idea of the general sinfulness of mankind describes something we can all recognize in our individual lives and in the tumultuous history of the world. We are ambivalent creatures, striving now this way and now that, full of promise and perfidy at the same time. But this is not a genetic defect nor some viral infection of the spirit. Such a sense of sinfulness is a reflection of the broken or incomplete aspect of the human situation. Sin is, however, a positive possibility, not just a lack of something. If sin is worth all the worry and if it is as powerful as we claim, then it must be something we can do; it cannot merely be something we forget or neglect to do. Nor can it be, in old-fashioned Fulton Sheen rhetoric, our capacity "to do nothing." Talking about omission is, in the realm of sin, more a copout than an insight. If sin is as destructive as the Christian tradition assures us, then it is something we must be able to recognize when we are doing it. It has to have a shape. Sin is not something that escapes our attention or that happens casually, although these concepts have often been employed with great effectiveness in preaching and writing about sin. This is to treat sin unfairly and to deny it an opportunity to reveal its true self. Sin is not a cowardly nightstalker, not a sniveling, deceptive presence nor an evil power outside of ourselves; sin is nothing if it is not our own.

Sin has suffered, as has general spirituality, from the implication that it has an existence separate from our own and that we can get entangled with it as with a spider's web. This is to diminish sin and to make it less possible for us to understand its essential nature as something, like anything powerful and important in life, we must do for ourselves. It remains a possibility for each one of us from the most apparently secure and saintly to the least advantaged outcast of the planet. Sin is not an impersonal force but a human accomplishment. Sin can have no meaning unless we pay it at least this much respect. That is why the flood of anthropological-psychological metaphors that have come to us in recent years serve to draw sin closer to our lives. We begin to grasp the meaning of sin when we feel it in ourselves.

Sinning, then, may be an experience more like loving than anything else. It describes a dynamic kind of presence toward ourselves and others that has powerful effects. While loving leads to life and its expansion, sinning diminishes and destroys life. As we can enlarge life through loving, so we can also take it away through sinning. Unless we are ready to face this honestly about ourselves, we will have only sentimental or abstract notions of sin. To sin, like to love, is something only we can do for ourselves, and something we do with all of ourselves. That we have the potency to be both lovers and sinners is reflected in the Scriptures where we are clearly described as being "at the same time just persons and sinners." Sinning is therefore related to the way we are, who we are, and what we do as consciously and as freely as we can manage.

All the other language about sin tends to distance it from us and make it more difficult for us to face and come to terms with what evil we are capable of committing. We

cannot speak of deadly sins except in living people. All the
devils and demons we have projected out from ourselves
as sources of sin through all of the centuries have merely
been psychological conveniences enabling us to objectify
what we did not want to gaze upon in ourselves. That is,
unfortunately, how some of the categories of sin have also
been used. We were able to match ourselves against the
stand of authority on whether we transgressed or not. That
simplified our understanding of and approach to life, but
it also denied us a deeper sense of what it means to be the
person who possesses such powerful ambivalent possibilities.
This also explains why it has always been so easy to be
moralistic and so difficult to be moral. Being moralistic
feasts on lip service and external conformity, but being
moral has to do with the things that actually take place
within us. Jesus constantly uses these contrasts about people
who say one thing with their mouths but keep their hearts
far from God; these, he suggests, are those hard enough of
heart to sin.

The question of what is right or wrong anymore comes
down to our judgment about our own extremely personal,
self-defining choices in this regard. How do we exercise
what freedom we can manage in this world? How can we
lay hold of the power either to love truly or to sin honestly?
Only adult people with some integrated sense of themselves
are capable of either in any full-blooded way. One of our
problems is our contemporary lack of passion for either
activity.

Our examination begins with ourselves and with an effort
to deepen our understanding of how we live from the inside
out. We possess ourselves as human beings when we are
able to examine our experience and to understand it with a
fair amount of accuracy. That means that we are able to
identify our feelings with the symbols that allow us to possess a sense of our wholeness. This has been given many

names in contemporary psychology; it is an idea as old as common sense and absolutely fundamental to the moral life. Only as we possess ourselves do we have a feeling for being subjects, makers of choices, and designers of our own lives. It is only as we sense our wholeness—even with the awareness of territory as yet unexplored rumbling beneath our feet—that we can in any sense be moral persons. This permits us to become better acquainted with our own motivation and to understand the galaxy of inclinations in our own inner space. We are not victims when we have the intelligence and sensitivity to come to terms with the varied aspects of our personal experience. The object of moral education is to make it possible for persons to sense the depths of themselves, to confront these, to make sense of them, and to understand them a little more with each passing year and so more fully to inhabit their own personalities.

Awareness is a chief characteristic of the moral person's activity. What I am suggesting is that growing adults move to a point where they can tell the difference between shame and guilt, when they can make a judgment between activity neurotically inspired or more fully and freely chosen. Not only that, but the moral person learns to take into account the vast bundle of unconscious dynamics whose tremors are felt throughout life. Perhaps we may be unable to see down deep enough to understand these parts of ourselves completely, but as morally aware individuals we are nonetheless able to gauge them by their effects, to recognize and take account of them as one would familiar sounds or blurred shapes seen on night passages. It is moral, in other words, to be able to take account of the dimensions of ourselves that we are still unable to see fully and to impose, insofar as we can, some informed subjective control on their role in our attitudes and actions. We become authors of our activity in this human fashion; otherwise we are just victims, never aware enough of ourselves to choose right or wrong decisively in anything.

For example, a man may drink heavily from time to time for psychological reasons of which he is originally quite unaware. He is, in effect, acting or living out the scenario composed in his unconscious. As he matures, he realizes the harmful effects of his drinking and also begins to understand the times when he is most likely to abuse alcohol. As he struggles against this difficulty, he may not penetrate fully the depths of his motivation to drink. He can, however, begin to sense that there is a cause inside himself and that he has a moral responsibility to deal with it even if he cannot fully identify it. He can go a long way in sensing its outlines, however, and in developing a practical, respectful working knowledge of how and when this aspect of his personality may assert or express itself. Moral maturity comes with a recognition of how he can sensibly order his life to minimize the dangers of being overwhelmed by these darker inner urges. He deals not with the devil but with himself, and morality is asserted as he more keenly and responsibly makes his way through life while taking into account and therefore better managing his drinking. This may lead him into other aspects of his attitudes toward himself—his moral life is lived in trying to understand and govern all that he is as responsibly as possible. His achievement may be an imperfect one. The chances are that this will be so; it will nonetheless be a moral life of acknowledged purpose rather than a blind struggle. He has become a subject rather than an object in life. His struggle against evil defines his pursuit of virtue.

That is one of the reasons that it is difficult to deal with sin on our own. It is hard to be a subject in life in the singular. We only come to understand ourselves in and through relationships with others and, in fact, this holds true for our sinfulness as well. Just as we need those poets and therapists who can understand our efforts to speak of our deepest longings and aspirations, those who are skilled enough to provide us with the words and interpretation that make sense out of these for us, so too we need mediators who will not necessarily impose an external meaning on our sinfulness but who will help us to accuse ourselves accurately of what we have done to hurt or to maim ourselves and others. Sin has, unfortunately, been something that we have had to think about largely by ourselves. Even though contemporary reflections on sin note its social character, there has not been much discussion about the fact that the realization of sin is also social in character and that, unaided by the insights and concerns of others, we are handicapped in understanding the dimensions of our own evil. We need someone to hear and therefore validate not only our goodness but also our badness. It is an aspect of redemption to live in the company of those who cannot only be sinned against by us but who also help us to articulate our sinfulness as a part of ourselves. Redemption has never been considered our own isolated struggle for righteousness with the Lord; the meaning of the Incarnation is that our salvation is mediated and continues to be mediated by all those who share the human condition with us. That is at the heart of the priest's mediatorship in the sacrament of penance.

The deadly sins, the offenses called capital, are difficult to understand unless we see them as the functions of persons who are truly subjects of life linked specifically with other human beings both for the realization and redemption of these sins. The traditional sins are not understood very well in the abstract. They are embarrassingly concrete in their implications, and they refer not to ways of thinking about ourselves but far more to ways of feeling about ourselves. They reflect our attitudes of presence in life and whether we make room either for the fullness of ourselves or for the presence of others. These sins shut us off so that

our sense of participation in life is limited and our appreciation of the dynamic meaning of revelation—which arises
from our capacity to share ourselves and to accept the gift
of others who would share themselves with us—is destroyed.

In pride, for example, we have feelings about our own
self-sufficiency, our own needs, priorities, and desires that
tend to leave little room around us for either sensing or
responding to other persons. Pride means that we are plea
bargainers for ourselves and that, to some extent, we can
understand what we are doing. We are making a choice
about the dimensions of our world, and just as we are reluc-
tant to leave it, so we also make it difficult for others to enter
it. We keep others out for our own selfish satisfaction; by
this we choose the isolated world of sin. This is why pride is
so destructive and why it can undermine relationships that
resemble friendship and love so disastrously. Pride is that
feeling for ourselves that rules out feeling for anyone else;
it is a decision to live only for ourselves. The proud person
refuses to see others as subjects in life with separate individual personalities that demand respect and concern.
Never breaking out of self-infatuation, the proud use people
for themselves in the kind of crude self-aggrandizement that
is at the heart of serious sin.

In the long run, persons guilty of pride withhold presence from others, not putting themselves out and not making any effort either to be sensitive or to understand the
psychological forces that may markedly influence their behavior. Pride in this virulent and sinful form chokes off life.
Pride is not, however, an accident. It is a way of life, a
style of presence chosen by ourselves. Pride distorts the
world, claiming it as our own and allowing us to become
the final judges and arbiters of practically all the significant
events in life. Pride is therefore isolating, a stubborn and
primal sin that places us beyond the relationships in which

we can come to terms with our appropriate guilt. Pride is the choice to live of, for, and by the self, to resist insight, and to avoid the expansion of the self that occurs in social sharing. Now that is a real sin, a killer because it makes it hard for us ever to come to life at all. And that is a sin we can feel and recognize breathing and heaving in our own personalities. It is sin enough to match the horror of which that concept is filled. It is a good sin to look at in particular in order to understand sin in general. And we only see it when we look straight at ourselves.

10

Can Anyone Sin Anymore?

The answer is yes but, as we have observed about all the important things in life, it takes concentration, sensitive perception, and a consolidated personal presence in order to do so. The most remarkable thing about life lies in the possibilities it holds up to us. These spring from the remarkable actions that are deeply expressive of human personality. On the one hand we have the power to love, to empty ourselves for the sake of others and through this long dying to selfishness to discover both ourselves and the secret of joy. It is not easy to love, and yet it remains at the apex of human achievement, the blinding accomplishment that we achieve through our total personalities. The other side of this possibility is, of course, that we can also choose selfishness and pull the covers of our own hardened self-concern across our hearts so that we knowingly live only for our own goals and interests. That is also a choice that can only be accomplished through the instrumentality of human personality. The dark side of ourselves, people are tempted to remark, and yet one with enormous power because we can freely write our signature on life in the bold strokes of sin. Sin is anything but for small children; like love it can only be found in a knowing adult.

There are several things we must keep in mind if we are to deepen our grasp of our potential for sin. Because sin is an adult accomplishment we do it when we know what we are doing and when we realize something about both the substance and the consequences of our behavior. Sinning is a function of the whole human personality. We must, in other words, be aware of ourselves as subjects and relate ourselves in life as subjects to others in order to be able to sin seriously. We recognize that there are many impediments to committing serious sin in life. People do not know themselves well, they never grow up, or they are blinded by impulses they do not recognize and cannot control. Even the reputedly stern moralists of the Roman Catholic Church have always recognized major impediments to the commission of serious sins. Even in what would be regarded as the most ancient and retrograde manuals of moral theology several chapters can be found detailing the factors that can diminish the freedom of the human will in action. Sinning, then, is serious business, and there are many ways to understand what might be labeled harmful behavior that is not sinful precisely because the individuals who author it neither possess themselves nor their actions sufficiently to claim them as their own responsibility.

A real sinner is a person who is acquainted with himself and who, oddly enough, is honest with himself. Sinners, in other words, do not perceive themselves or others as objects. Because they have some feeling for the wonder of human personality and human individuation, they are not naïve about the raw materials necessary for serious sin.

One of the prime characteristics of serious sinners is that their perception of themselves and of others is fairly clear and not distorted in any major way. We react to the world

as we perceive it, and the more accurately we sense its outlines as they match those of reality, the more realistic and
alert we can be in all of our activities. Sensitive and accurate perception is a predisposition to being a subject in
life. When people view the world in a distorted way, their
capacity for weighty virtue or serious sin is thereby diminished. Reacting to the world as they perceive it, they are
lost in a universe of private meanings that take away their
ability to discriminate between what is true and what is
false in themselves and in those around them. True sinners
see things fairly clearly; they can call a spade a spade. That
is the remarkable accuracy of outlook that is possessed by
a person capable of choosing to sin seriously. Only an individual who does perceive the world and the self clearly
can have a conscience that may be transgressed. Sinners
hear the message of their conscience, the dictates that tell
them when and how they are violating the rights or personalities of others. Serious sinning is never a casual activity. It takes a close look at the sinner and those who are
affected by the sins. Sinners, in other words, make no mistakes in making their mistakes. They are more like careful
assassins who choose their targets and know their skill well
than like accidental fumblers who hurt others merely by
mischance.

Such an inspection of sin helps us to realize how seriously
we need to take ourselves in life. If this power of ours is the
other side of our potential for love, then this is the contemporary fight of the gods. In reaching that point in life
in which we sense and exercise our power to love or to hurt,
we achieve a feeling for how deep the mystery of being
alive genuinely is. There is no sin to speak of, however, if
we live only on the surface and never look beneath our behavior or ever understand our power for life. We are the
lead characters in this struggle; the myth turns out to be the

story of our own lives. Everything is at stake as we face the choices between loving and sinning.

Another realization available to genuine sinners is that evil is not outside of themselves. We may seem to experience evil as something alien to us; that is why the devil has gotten so much due. Objectifying our own capacity for evil separates it from us. While this is understandable psychologically, it is hazardous as far as living a sharply edged existence goes. As long as we do not admit evil into our own selves we can arrange life as a battle between ourselves and the malign forces around us. That is a relatively primitive way of peopling the stage of our existence, however, and persisting in this construction of life makes it difficult for us to come to terms with our own existence. The sinner does not think that there is some strange voice piped into his head that speaks to him regularly about what is right and wrong. Sinners come to realize—as indeed all adults sooner or later must—that this voice, which can seem disembodied, is actually their own. Sinners take life seriously enough to appreciate the inner vaults of personality in which echo our internal debates about the direction and meaning of our lives. Sinners, like lovers, have developed a sense of oneness about experience so that they can locate the source of what they do well within the borders of their own personalities. They have indeed put away childish things and look now at things as adults. That is the terrifying aspect of our capacity for sin. Sin is something that only we can accomplish. It is not something done to us or something into which we are tricked by another; we make our way into it on our own.

It also follows that the better related we are to other persons, the more aware we will be of our potential for sinfulness. This may seem paradoxical, and yet it is obvious that as we genuinely draw close to others we sense more about ourselves and about them with greater honesty and

perception. We are more true to ourselves as we draw closer
to other persons. We can, at that close range, understand
more of the impact we have on other persons even in our
smallest daily relationships with them. It takes closeness to
another to realize the implications of our presence in someone else's life. Here we begin to realize how much we affect
them even by the attitudes we leave unspoken. It is difficult
for persons to understand the consequences of their personal behavior unless they can witness these in the lives of
other persons who are affected strongly by them. Sinners
do things not to anonymous mobs but to living persons.
They know that they are hurting, that they are depriving
others of life, that they are taking something away from
other human beings. That is why serious sinners can experience real guilt; they can attach the consequences of their
actions to their source in themselves. They know clearly
what they do because they are close enough to other persons to attune their own reactions to them in a fine and
delicate manner. They can hear and feel what they do.

Authentic sinners have also developed a capacity for
judgment, for understanding when they are present fully in
their actions and when they are not. When we sin seriously
we innervate our actions so that we can truthfully claim
them as our own. We understand, in other words, that it is
precisely in this situation that *I* act, that it is here that *I* am
indeed joined to reality with the fullness of myself. Sinning
is, if anything, a heightened moment of personal awareness.
It is anything but a blind and unknowing stab in the dark.
We have a sense of power when we sin because the transaction has deadly effectiveness. Perhaps that power is one
of its attractions. We know what we have done and we
realize that we did it for and by ourselves.

Serious sinners appreciate the moment of choice that occurs in genuine sin. They realize that this is a moment of
self-definition, a strange and negative aspect of revelation

through which they make a statement about themselves and their values and goals. We cannot possibly sin unless we are able to weigh the values in the situation, unless we have some clear vision of the things that are risked and the potential for hurt that is always involved. Genuine sinners realize that it does not make much difference what their actions look like on the outside, because sin can easily inhere in what can seem to be innocent and wholesome activities. A kiss betrayed Jesus, and similar signals have betrayed other people all through history. The kiss that is given by the person who withdraws his own presence from the event—who knowingly understands that the symbol he makes is false and intentionally deceptive—understands the role of intention in genuine sinfulness. There is a person who knows how to sin.

Authentic sinners also understand that they do something to themselves in the process of choosing evil. When we are serious about our activities we know that we are lessened by such a choice and that we are hardened by the act of sinning itself. We know these things and yet we still choose to act in this way or that way—to cheat, defame, or deceive —making ourselves vulnerable to the living effects of sin. They are not encrustations resembling barnacles on our souls. They are more like a deepened sense of direction, a guidance system to which we commit ourselves more firmly through our repeated actions. We are involved, in other words, in a spiritual suicide when we commit serious sin. We sink more deeply into ourselves because we have to live with what we have chosen. What we have chosen is a world just for ourselves with as little room as possible for the presence of anybody else. That world grows more intense as we repeatedly choose to live in it. If it is difficult for us to escape, it is because we have knowingly made it that way by ourselves. Hardening of the heart goes into any sin that genuinely deserves the name.

One of the ways, in fact, through which we can make a judgment about our sinfulness is through observing whether and how we are trying to love other people. As long as we are still trying to reach out to others, as long as we can still feel for them as separate from us, we are not committed fully to nor lost in sinfulness. We are a long way from being serious sinners precisely because love and sin cannot coexist in personality. Most persons are involved in the struggle to love others as truthfully and richly as they can. They may have their difficulties in doing this, but as they continue to do their best, they place themselves in opposition to the world of sin. We cannot be concerned about others and commit serious sin at the same time. Anybody who tries to be a friend, anybody who takes other persons seriously, thereby limits severely his or her capacity to sin gravely. Any signs of unselfishness are indications that we have not chosen sin over against the grace that is evidenced in a loving life.

It is clear that not many persons are genuine sinners. Life, for most persons, is a process of trying to overcome or temper what psychologist David Bakan once described as the agentic in ourselves through achieving communion with others. The essence of a Christian life lies still in the steady effort to break out of ourselves in order to make continuing contact in a loving way with other persons. The agentic will to selfishness, to an individualized sense of power and isolation, destroys us until it is overcome by a will to communion through sharing ourselves with other persons. In this struggle we deal with the two-faced power of loving and sinning. Most people want to do the right thing, and they are helped immeasurably when they realize that life is a long struggle to understand and use our power to love and enlarge each other's lives.

Just as sinners must have a serious understanding of the consequences of their behavior, so we also need a clear view of what we can accomplish through love. We take ourselves seriously when we understand how caught up we are in the recurring themes of the whole of Scripture. We stand always by the tree of life that can also be a tree of death. There we sense how life involves us in the mystery of fall-redemption in our recurring experiences of death and resurrection together. As we work through these enormous realities we begin to realize the significance and the startling power of our human experience. We are neither sinners nor saints if we are estranged from our own experience of life. That is why we are invited to plunge ourselves into our humanity and to taste these mysterious and ambivalent challenges through which we discover the meaning of being persons.

We can no longer live by the descriptions other people give to our lives nor by the advice or moral principles that others construct around us. The great trial and expression of the Christian life comes as we understand its common raw materials from which we forge an identity that fits the power of life and death that we have as human beings. Above all, we understand that we cannot be passive to life, and we grasp that to sin or to love requires passion, a wholehearted commitment of ourselves to the experience of our own lives and times. Nothing happens when we wait, as all too many do, for life to deliver its rewards. Can anyone sin anymore? Yes, as many as there are who can love, who possess enough of themselves to make a lasting mark on life. The worst thing is that so much of life goes down the drain unmarked by either loving or sinning.

11

Some Real Sins

Some contemporary thinkers about moral problems who have made an effort to understand the complexities of human behavior have been accused of doing away with sin. Indeed, moral theologian Charles E. Curran was once introduced at a conference with the scriptural quote, "Behold him who takes away the sin of the world." It is a stylish and oversimplified way of not dealing with the truth of the matter; it is the kind of thing frustrated people say when confronted with ambiguity. No one can think seriously about human life for any length of time, however, without realizing that we possess a terrible power to do wrong and, far from doing away with sin, that as we learn more about human personality we actually begin to understand how and when we can sin. False notions of sin and guilt have, in fact, been among our greatest obstacles in developing a more reliable awareness of our own capacity for committing sin. There are many things that we can do that are harmful to us and to others. These are things about which we do have a choice, things to which we can say yes or no. Our contemporary moral awareness depends on whether we believe that we have a choice even about having a choice about what we do in life.

People who are honest with themselves even for short periods realize that they can do hurtful things, that they can choose the darkness rather than the light, that they can turn away from what they know to be right and inoculate themselves against the promptings of the Spirit. The immunization that selfishness gives us allows us to pass through life without being affected by the problems or sufferings of others. We can remain unresponsive by choice and, when we are, we may glimpse the harmful consequences of which we are the cause.

Sin is not an imaginary phenomenon, nor some artifact from a civilization of long-forgotten gods. It remains a lively possibility, with deadly consequences for all of us. Sin, by its very nature, is not outside of us; it exists in and through the deliberate actions of human beings. It is a special human power, the shattering capability that human beings alone possess. When we examine our sinfulness we do not count up individual wrong actions. We rather search for a sense of how much we are alive, of how much, in other words, within our possibilities and liabilities, we affirm or deny ourselves and other persons.

Contemporary lists of sins abound. They are not really very different from the kinds of wrong that have been recorded all through history. In each era, however, persons take a fresh look at old sins and sometimes bind them in new casings. There is not much new about sin, but there are new ways of understanding sinfulness, new and better ways of grasping our awesome power to give or withhold life. If we think, for example, of the Commandments, we find a wide variety of attitudes and behaviors which allow us to understand these ancient precepts. The following are merely suggestions that provide us with some operational ways of

examining ourselves regularly in order to come to terms with
our sinfulness.

"Then God delivered all these Commandments: *I, the
Lord, am your God. . . . You shall not have other gods besides me. . . .*"

Carving idols is not very fashionable in the modern world,
but raising false images of God is not unusual at all. Human
beings are led to worship various unsatisfactory goals, such
as power and celebrity, and these can be recognized as the
hollow deities of the day. False gods are raised whenever
we propagate a notion about God that misrepresents or
distorts him. Such, for example, are the ideas of a vengeful
God, breathing fire and puffing with righteous indignation,
a haunting specter glaring across the edge of history in order
to consume his creatures in a final incineration of divine
justice.

Scaring people to death about their creator is a classic
method of raising graven images, popular because this is the
kind of God that enables its sponsors to exercise control over
the lives of other human beings. It not only gives the wrong
idea about God but also notably distorts our ideas about
ourselves, our lives, and even what constitutes the serious
possibility of sin. Any misinterpretation of God and his works
provides a way of violating this abiding Commandment.
We do it when we make God our good-luck charm or the
one to turn to only in times of danger; it is blasphemy to
make him a God of battle and destruction who will help us
vanquish our enemies. God is falsely represented whenever
we generate neurotic guilt in persons in order to make them
feel that they can never please the God who gave them life
and who gave his Son so that they could have life to the
full. These false gods do not live in pagan temples but, all
too often, in supposedly Christian churches, kept there by
fearful ministers who are sect members rather than be-

lievers. Quite often, with quite clear reflection and determination, they design this God for their own purposes.

A false image of God is raised to people whenever we so exclusively focus on him that we demean or lessen our ability to see and to understand human experience. Some people seem to be worried very much about God, his health, and his whereabouts, and whether he sleeps well at night. They so emphasize his need for worship and attention that they feel that all human enterprise must be spurned in order to accomplish this. This is, however, a dangerously false and deceiving God who would have us look beyond the only experience that we can deal with, that of our human exchange with each other. It is a false and cruel picture of God—a sinful one indeed—that makes it seem that loving each other and loving him necessarily divides our hearts. This builds a conflict nobody needs into life, confuses persons, and, in the long run, does a disservice to God himself. Whatever we know of him, and however inadequately we know it, comes from the revelation communicated in and through human experience. It is all that we have and, in the Christian vision, God is not an arrogant father demanding submission but a tender lover seeking us out even in our sins with foregiveness and understanding.

Some people are worried that if we gave up the idea of an all-just God, the world will go to pieces or the Churches will suffer a loss in attendance or that people will simply not behave themselves anymore. These are the motivations that lead people into the contemporary idolatry of perpetuating the image of a wrathful and distant God who hungers always for sacrifice rather than mercy. It is sinful to present that kind of God to persons, especially at formative stages in their lives, because this makes it almost impossible for them ever to find or understand the God of Love later on. God, in sum, is a lover, not an administrator.

"You shall not take the name of the Lord, your God, in vain. . . ."

We are familiar with the traditional mode of defining sacrilege and how defaming or making ill use of temples, altars, and other sacred places and persons is a prime violation of God and his special symbols. Contemporary persons are, however, aware of the fact that God's handiwork does not end at the chapel door nor the edge of the altar; it extends rather to all of creation. Sacrilege is, therefore, a possibility whenever we knowingly abuse something of God's creation. This includes our recent insights into our plundering of God's good earth, of ill using our resources. It also includes trespassing on the sacred territory of another's personality. We can do this in many ways.

We can, for example, mislead people about understanding themselves, not only giving them the wrong image of God but also the wrong image of the way their own personality works. This is to abuse God's handiwork, to distort rather than to expand what it means to be human. Sometimes this is accomplished through the invocation of religious sentiments to manipulate persons into certain responses through making them unnecessarily experience fear, guilt, or shame about certain actions. This deliberate estrangement of persons from their own human experience may be the prime sacrilege of the day. It is almost always committed for what people construe to be the best of reasons. These are apparently religious in nature and, although they result in crippling human beings, they are imposed "for their own good" or "for the sake of their salvation." These include the many damaging manipulations of persons that have occurred throughout history. If we confine ourselves only to its ecclesiastical varieties, we can observe the dangerous perfectionism that so exalted the intellectual and mechanical in our behavior and so alienated people from a full sense of themselves. This is what generated the classic

Catholic conflict of obsessiveness and sentenced so many human beings to a lifelong pursuit of trying to please a dour God who remained beyond all pleasing.

This sacrilege is inflicted on people who are misled about the nature of love, when, for example, they are told that it is dangerous for them to have affection for other human beings because this dilutes in some way their love for God. This manipulation of persons for good ends has caused as much suffering as almost anything else in the history of the world because, so informed by seemingly authoritative figures, good and trusting people have tried earnestly to escape their humanity in order to find God. The pain of this search and the distortion of personality that has resulted from it may be seen in the scars and bitterness of many persons' lives. Their chance at happiness was ruined when they entrusted their persons to directors or spiritual gurus who did not have the slightest idea of what they were doing. This hurt is easy to inflict, but even a lifetime may not heal it.

This is what happens whenever anybody exerts excessive control over human personality in order to save people from life and its attendant dangers. Such controllers end up denying people even the opportunity of a free and full life. While this is done under the banners of "doing good" to others, it almost always ends up doing ill to them instead. These do-gooders who do harm are a lively and constant group, never far out of sight and in temporary and strategic retreat at best.

Sacrilege occurs whenever we oppress other persons, whether they are members of our own family, our students, or our fellow citizens. We can oppress them indirectly, by going along with the oppression insisted upon by others, and by neglecting to engage ourselves in the fight for their fuller liberation for life. There is a special obligation shared by teachers, politicians, and churchmen in regard to the liberation of persons for a fuller life. The failure to engage ourselves in this struggle—and this can be a deliberate stance —is to choose the role described by Thomas Merton as that of a "guilty bystander." We are guilty in this role, not to meet our masochistic needs, but when we choose not to act and when we choose to look the other way when life is being choked out of persons around us through injustice and manipulation. It is easy to let people get killed and to refuse, with rationalizations aplenty, to try to save them or even stand by them. "Things have always been this way," "You'll never change human nature": familiar phrases in the contemporary sacrilege of assenting to the disfigurement rather than the enlargement of human personality.

This was forcefully expressed by the streetwise novelist Jimmy Breslin when I asked him where he saw evil in the contemporary world. He responded, "Bribery is the worst thing; that's the worst thing. It's just terrible. Boy, it's—" and he paused, sighing wistfully, "Very few bribes go untaken. A lot of lives get ruined that way. That's why I see the devil in life, ruining people that way. I believe in the devil. Not as a lascivious woman waiting to get you on your way home from work. No, it's in things like bribery. Extortion is in there. That's an extension of bribery, and it's a hell of a lousy crime. The act of bribing a policeman; it is an unenforceable law to try to stop that. They can get around it in so many ways. The ordinary guy, he can be bribed and so he can extort. There's an ingredient of evil there that's going to hurt them all."

It may seem discouraging to survey a world in which so many sacrileges, so many assaults on the human spirit and on human possibilities seem to abound. And yet we participate in this sacrilege if we do not involve ourselves in improving the world in which we live. We not only reject sin, but we also concretely love our neighbor whenever, even in a very small but positive way, we step forward in the name of treating persons more humanly. That is what it takes to discover the chief ingredient of the good life.

Sacrileges are also committed by those persons who mindlessly offer the world shallow and misleading opportunities of liberation. This is a way of selling human beings short, of manipulating them for political or other ends, and of involving them in experiences that do not deliver the redemption they promise. There are recurrent themes in the fads that are presented to people in the name of liberation. There is almost always just enough truth in these schemes to make it all seem plausible. For example, the still-reverberating sexual revolution promised a new world of pleasure and freedom to persons who would cut themselves loose from most of the constraints that could be described as at least semi-Victorian. The rationalizations for indulging in an impulsive life have been designed to make it easy for people to abandon former standards or to escape from oppressive institutions like marriage and old-fashioned virtues like fidelity. There is a special sacrilege in promising people so much of life and delivering such meager and ultimately unsatisfying realities. The harvest of disillusionment and unhappiness, the emptiness experienced by so many people who thought that they were finally finding sensual liberation: these are some of the effects of this sacrilegious behavior.

There is also a sacrilege involved in refusing to read the signs of our times, that distinct Christian obligation without which it is so difficult to understand either ourselves or our particular part of history. We can cultivate our gardens or collect our trivia and avoid learning about ourselves or the times in which we live. It is sacrilegious, I suggest, not to make the effort to read and understand our civilization, its direction, its values, and our relationship to improving it. It is also sacrilegious not to read the signs in ourselves in our failure to come to grips with our own personal experience.

We may know, for example, that something is rumbling inside of us, resonating in our unconscious, but we do not look carefully at it, and we know ourselves less as a result. We can choose not to know ourselves and so choose a special darkness and death rather than light and resurrection. This is to turn away from the responsibility of an authentic self-possession and to be diminished and disfigured as a result. The effects of this sacrilege show up in many places in our lives: in our friendships, in our way of doing business, and in our whole way of participating in our time and place. It is always a sacrilege to substitute things like activity for the kind of reflective contemplation on our lives and purpose that mark us as adult and responsible human beings.

"Remember to keep holy the Sabbath Day."

We fail to keep the Sabbath holy, not merely by laboring on it or by failing to attend religious services, but by not taking a religious response to life seriously. It is one thing to go through the external actions of worshiping God; it is very different, however, to take religion seriously enough to try to integrate it in our lives and to make it our own so that our behavior flows from our total personality rather than from just a part of it. We can never keep the Sabbath holy if we choose to stick with a religion that is itself immature and therefore incapable of reflecting praise to our maker. We dishonor the Sabbath on all the days of our lives when we are content with the literal, fundamentalistic faith that offers us security but denies us the more profound experience of truly believing. God is only worshiped by whole persons, and a faith that is fit for children is hardly resonant enough of human experience to be used by adults. We violate the Sabbath when we fail to grow religiously or when we hold back from helping others to grow toward a fuller grasp and possession of religious belief. It is a violation of God's Sabbath when we think that we can so restrict worship that many legitimate and significant forms of human expressions

can never be brought into the liturgy. Only a true desecrater
of the Sabbath would think that the dance or drama was
inappropriate in the worship of God or that new music or
new symbols might offend the Lord. The Sabbath is kept
holy when we worship God with our wholeness and when
we are not afraid to bring to the altar a full measure of our
human accomplishments and possibilities.

"Honor your father and your mother. . . ."

It is clear that being obedient is a virtue but that it is not
the only good thing associated with reverence toward our
parents. Nor can this Commandment be thought of only in
terms of our relationship to our mothers and fathers. Honor-
ing our parents underscores the whole realm of human relationships, telling us that they are essentially connected
with the religious experience of life. Any deliberate choice
not to be with or in the human condition with our brothers
and sisters is a way of rejecting relationship as our essential
moral mode. This is expressed, for example, through hardness of heart, that ancient biblical sin that has never disappeared. We are hard of heart when we do not listen to
other persons, when, for example, we merely make a check
mark or write off their feelings or concerns as of little importance. We are made for relationships; it is only the self-
centered heart that can choose to live and beat only for
itself. That is to reject our human heritage and our best possibilities; it is a dark will to isolated death, and it kills love
before it can start. It is not, regrettably, a rare choice; it is
the will to self at its most intense and deadly.

We are hard of heart when we oversimplify the motivations and activities of other persons. I recall an enthusiastic
priest, deep in various contemporary movements, shaking
his head about some of his brother priests who had chosen
to get married. Very confident of his judgments and
very sure of his holiness, he proclaimed to me at lunch one
day, "They have simply lost their faith, they have no faith

anymore. . . ." It was all very simple and very consoling to this priest, who prided himself so much on having kept his faith. Unfortunately, his interpretation of the actions of men we both knew was cheap and inaccurate. He had no understanding of the struggles and difficulties with which these priests had labored in order to make their decisions. Far from losing their faith, most of them had deepened it in the process, because they took it and themselves seriously. It is easy to be hard of heart and to judge everybody else from our own viewpoint on their moral, religious, or any other kind of behavior. It is easy and it is almost always wrong; that is terminal hardness of heart at its worst.

Hard-heartedness is recognized by the rejection of the effort to open ourselves in understanding to other persons. Understanding always demands a positive effort. It is not a simple process, and it cannot be achieved by nodding passively at life. Hardness of heart occurs whenever we refuse to empty ourselves of our own concerns so that we can make room for the cares of others in our own reflections. Such an attitude rejects involvement in the incarnational mystery; it represents a refusal to die even briefly in order to make room for other persons in life. It is a knowing sin, a sin committed by a clear choice of the self over others.

We are hard-hearted whenever we refuse the invitation of love, an invitation that comes our way far more often than we sometimes think. Whenever we respond out of fear or because we want to keep ourselves clear of any involvement with other persons, we clearly choose not to love. We choose not to respond to others in need. We speak from armored hearts that we save only for ourselves in order to avoid the only kind of trouble worth having in life, that which comes with love.

"You shall not kill."

There are many ways to murder people, and only a few of them are by way of guns, knives, or other instruments of destruction. We kill people when we refuse to believe in them or when we do not make the effort to trust in them or hope for them or to give them some experience of our love and concern. Withdrawing or refusing to share these things with other persons is a way of depriving them of life, of cutting its possibility off early, and of refusing them the nourishment they need in order to penetrate the meaning of their own existence. This is frequently a deliberate act, one that flows from our own unwillingness to give much of ourselves away. There is, of course, no other way that we can love people, no other way to tap this fundamental energy of the spirit. We cannot love indirectly nor merely by dreaming about it. We pay for it by what we yield up of our own lives for the sake of others. That requirement has never changed. We can choose not to be with people and to live only for ourselves and our own isolated concerns. We may not notice how slowly this becomes our habitual attitude, and we may not let ourselves see how deadly it can be in its effects. This is not only a way of murdering other people, you see, but it is also a way of dying at our own hands; many people, moaning for the love they do not have, have only a dim realization of their responsibility for the situation.

We also kill other persons by restricting their freedom, by binding them psychologically in a fashion analagous to the way Indian children may be bound as infants and so deformed for life. Freedom is a necessary condition for a truly human existence. Freedom is sometimes thought to be a dangerous kind of weapon, something like the nuclear bomb, and so self-approving people justify limiting the experience of freedom they allow to other persons. It is so dangerous and therefore so reasonable to restrict it. At times persons who are charged with allowing people to experience as much freedom as possible, the freedom of the sons of God, restrict the freedom of others the most. Many religious leaders, for example, have preached counsels of fear about what people would do if they were allowed to be free or make up their own minds on certain issues. We kill people by giving them all the answers all the time because we thereby effectively prevent them from getting in touch with the core of themselves. Such persons can be crippled for life by this cruel process, made dead to themselves and to their own life possibilities. And, sadly enough, these killings are carried out often by people who deem themselves altruistic or benevolent.

We can be murderous by refusing to give up the killing games that some people adopt as their style of life. Truth, St. Augustine wrote once, can be murderous. So it is when it is used as a weapon against others in order to intimidate or shame them. We kill others by not respecting their frailty or their need for their own defenses or their need to grow in accord with their own inner timetable. We are murderous when we refuse to give up the hostile games of childhood and insist on revenge against those who have wronged us, and on getting even, settling old scores, or hurting people in any vengeful way. We can be murderous when we deny people room in which to find themselves, when we are so self-absorbed that we cannot sense or will not sense the presence of others around us in life. We kill others by not taking them seriously and by never making our persons available to them; we do it when we feed them clichés and prevent them from asking the questions that lead to their own true self-discovery. I am reminded of the self-assured spiritual director in an old-fashioned seminary who was always indignant that the students who came to him had problems. I recall his wrath and his famous quote to an offending young seminarian one day: "Who do you think you are to have an identity crisis!" That attitude, in many variations, constitutes one of the great killers of all time.

We kill other people when we are not genuine with them, when, for example, we lack the strength of character to face squarely with them some conflict or difficulty we are experiencing with them. We can kill people by being passive-aggressives, by withdrawing our presence and slipping away to leave them in their misery or pain, confused and defeated not so much by an active assault as by a fearful retreat out of their lives. However we do it, the results are just as deadly. These are the deadly things that are within our power to do to each other. Sometimes we only let ourselves half realize what we are doing. Perhaps that diminishes some of our responsibility, but it does not spare the other person a full measure of suffering. There may be many accidental deaths caused by our failure to realize the power of life and death we actually have over others. We cannot afford to be like Tom and Daisy Buchanan of *The Great Gatsby*, "careless people."

"You shall not commit adultery. . . . You shall not covet your neighbor's house. . . . You shall not covet your neighbor's wife. . . ."

These commands are clearly related to the style and reality of our relationships with others. We violate these Commandments by the simple refusal to take ourselves and our commitments in life seriously. We can commit deadly sins by neglecting to acknowledge or by refusing to look at the consequences of our actions on those around us. Insisting on being No. 1, justifying any and all activities that gratify us personally, lead us to violate the lives, possessions, and relationships of others in a reckless and destructive manner. We may blind ourselves to some extent to these consequences but, if we are honest, we can see that a failure in keeping faith with the truth of ourselves and our own possibilities leads us easily to commit these sins. There is far more involved here than sexual transgression. It is related rather to the sacrilege mentioned in earlier paragraphs of this chapter. These are the evils that erupt around us when we will not break away from the narrow viewpoint through which we judge everything in terms of our own needs or our own concerns. This is what happens when we back away from commitments or never involve ourselves in appreciating their meanings or their implications. When we live solely inside of ourselves there is no barrier and no concern for understanding others that may limit our doing whatever we want at any moment that we feel like it. This violates ourselves at the same time that it so crushingly violates the lives of others. Call the sin stealing or sexual thievery; they are species of the same poisoned fruit.

"You shall not steal. . . . You shall not bear false witness against your neighbor. . . ."

In an age in which dishonesty has been raised to new and unanticipated levels, these Commandments need almost national reflection. It has become so easy to take what is not ours in an age of the glorified ripoff, to disrespect the property to which we have no right, to cheat and count it clever, that we may need to examine ourselves very closely on the moral points that have grown sadly dull. It is clear that taking the possessions of others is stealing and that it is a serious matter. What is insidious is the rationalization of appropriating another person's property that has so casually become a part of the thinking of affluent America. It is merely one aspect of not taking life and other persons seriously, of living in a protoplasmic universe in which one can float along almost forever without moral responsibilities or concerns.

There are many less dramatic ways, however, in which we steal the property of others. We can do it, for example, when we never have a thought of our own and when, as a result, we live by clichés or slogans fashioned by other persons in order to give some kind of shape to our own life. We steal whenever we do not think through a problem but appropriate someone else's solution, plastering it on the outside of our lives as we would on a billboard but never really making it a part of ourselves. We steal when we borrow existence from others, draining them of their energies and refusing to make ourselves fully accountable for our behavior. We steal whenever we refuse to find and live by the truth of our own existence.

Many offenses against these Commandments can be described in terms of hypocrisy and pretense of all kinds, in fact in any of the actions in which we choose appearances over reality. This affects many things besides the politics that have been the focus of our moral attention in recent years. It can happen in religion, for example, when we act piously instead of being genuinely religious, when we recite creeds but do not integrate our beliefs into some pattern that gives direction and meaning to our behavior in life. We do it whenever we say what is expected by others rather than what arises genuinely from our own experience. We are hypocritical when we fail to be consistent in our attitudes or behavior, constantly shifting in order to achieve popularity or the approval of other persons. We are hypocritical, in other words, whenever we neglect our own character and choose to live a hollowed-out existence in which personal development has not taken place.

We are hypocritical when we choose to be moralistic rather than moral, mouthing what sounds religious or ethical but detaching it from any connection with our own experience or behavior. Hypocrisy is involved whenever we participate in handing on a false interpretation of life to other persons. This can be in the form of a shallow, self-conscious, and self-serving religious program, the kind that has become somewhat popular in modern-day evangelization. It can occur if we offer an insubstantial or cynical interpretation of life to our children, students, or to our parishioners. We are hypocritical whenever we refuse to call things by their right names. This not only bears false witness to the meaning of life, but also proclaims the falsity of our own presence in life.

Hypocrisy may be the deadliest of all sins; other sins are associated in some way with this refusal to be genuine, with this withdrawing of our true presence in order to stay at a safe distance from life and from others. Most of these sins are committed to protect ourselves from life and to save ourselves from its hurts or embarrassments, and yet, in one of the perennially fresh truths of Christianity, the more we try to save ourselves this way the more surely we lose ourselves. Most of our sins are connected with trying to avoid the experience of death that is so necessary for any kind of resurrecting Christian experience of life. Sin is death because it represents a choice not to live fully and to deny the chance for life to others.

12

A Sense of Passion

The most profound alienation produced in this century is that which, in the name of progress, has estranged us from a serious sense and appreciation of what it means to be human. We have, indeed, struggled, not so directly with our humanity, but to eliminate or triumph over the incidental evidence of the human in our lives. Living in the human situation has come to be considered a disease from which at all costs we must be cured. If theological abstractions bar us from a feel for life on one end of the vital spectrum, our own pseudoconcerns for a new perfectionism in human imagery have blocked our way on the other. It is no wonder that people find it difficult to define or to make moral decisions. The problem is not that moral principles have disappeared but that our personal capacity to relate them to our lives effectively has been crippled because of our own clouded identity, our own gradually achieved remoteness from a sense of living in and through the truth of our personalities. Possessing ourselves less surely, confused about our goals or the dimensions of the good or even the bearable life, and uneasy with our limitations, we feel morally impotent.

Now, it might be fashionable, in some revivalistic style, to condemn the human race for getting itself into such a situation; it might be possible to scare or otherwise manipulate some people into what we used to call repentance by summoning the echoes of a hellfire religious tradition. This would be unfortunate and ill-advised if only on the basis of our poor track record throughout history in scaring people into the virtuous life. Such approaches are part of the problem because they do not take people or their lives seriously. It is also unnecessary to condemn people for vague and unspecified crimes of unworthiness. Too many people are already plagued with anxiety about their existence, the outline of which they sometimes manage to catch in the quiet moment or two that our culture occasionally provides. The problem is not lessened by making people feel bad; too many of them do not feel good about themselves, their lives, or their work; they are simply unhappy. And they are that way not because they are such colossal, conscious sinners but because they have such difficulties in discovering something deeper and richer about their life experience.

Human beings merit something better than pity, something more on the order of the mature compassion that reaches out to help them come to grips with the truth of their lives. It is not good enough, in other words, just to get mad at people and to lead a golden-trumpeted crusade for better moral behavior. It is, first of all, vital to hear their muffled and disguised cries for a better identity—a better chance to feel what it means to be human—and to support and work for their liberation and personal development as determinedly as possible. Only as people have the opportunity to mature can they achieve a more developed moral sense. It is impossible to be moral without first understanding what it means to be alive. The marvel is that everyone has abundant raw material in his own experience—life does not leave anyone out—that waits for sensitive illumination and interpretation by those individuals and institutions capable of delivering a sense of meaning to it. There is no point in getting morally indignant at people for being fumblingly human. What they truly need is a clear place in a cluttered culture in which to discover who they are.

And there is little justification in railing against those favorite targets, the materialism and abundance of America, unless we can at the same time provide some vision and encouragement for more deeply experienced human lives. That is the key, but many moral educators apparently do not have the subtlety of judgment to understand it. They prefer the old abstractions or the even older preachy harangue; these are, after all, far more familiar and easier to deliver. Some prefer a new ethical situationism which, while headed in the right direction of an appreciation for concrete individual lives, gets popularly translated into a fuzzy and romantic rationalization of most things on the basis of love. That is fine except that so many people have such a vague understanding of what love itself means. If sin is the other side of love, then a thorough exploration of what it does mean to love others is a prerequisite for living responsibly in one's own situation. The new morality suffers, not because it lacks the right instincts, but because it proposes a kind of sophisticated moral self-judgment that most people are still unable to make about themselves. One is tempted to call it a morality ahead of most people's time, not because it is intrinsically wrongheaded, but because it depends on the kind of maturity that most people have not as yet achieved. It is, in effect, disintegrated from the average person's experience just as surely as an overintellectualized theological category can be. A clinical morality of our individual lives remains for most persons a goal toward which they are still making a somewhat wandering journey.

One of the basic challenges to moral educators is to free persons from the enslaving or short-sighted value systems in which they find themselves. Indeed, moralists could learn a great deal from psychologist B. F. Skinner in this regard. They prefer, of course, to criticize him and to make him a symbol for our new inhumanity. That is part of the righteous indignation-scapegoat syndrome through which we feel morally relieved if we can blame someone, anybody, for our woes. Skinner, however, is benign and compassionate toward persons and wants, if possible, to help them save themselves from avoidable errors and mistakes in life. He quite rightly directs our attention to our environment, the world we create for ourselves to live in. We shape our buildings, the old saying goes, and then our buildings shape us. Psychoarchitecture underscores the way in which we build our own controlling environments and, with some insight and planning, the way we can design them for better human functioning. Skinner's thesis is, in fact, startlingly moral and simple: We can do something about ourselves and our discontents, but only if we do it as consciously and clearly as possible. And we begin with the world we fashion as a setting for our moral lives.

Human beings need, in other words, living space in which they can feel the truth of their existence and in which they can rediscover a passion for life itself. They will then be freed not only to love but also to sin far more clearly and decisively. We are not describing a new Utopia wherein we will all be restored to an undefiled state of grace. This is a simple and more earthy vision of a place in which we will re-establish enough contact with ourselves both to love and to sin in a more full-bodied way, a place in which life will be seen not as an illness but as the highly imperfect location of our incarnation and redemption in the human mode. We are not going to build Walden Two and save ourselves from our sins; all we need is a more human setting that gives us a chance to feel what it means to be alive before we die. One of the reasons for our present cultural preoccupation with death is related to our frustration about getting into life before it slips by like a bus we were waiting for but still missed. Living with passion makes it possible for us both to be lovers and sinners once again; our main woe is that we are neither in any satisfactory way. We do not feel alive enough for the richer experiences of existence; that is why people speak of this as an amoral rather than an immoral age.

Indeed, the Watergate phenomenon—which we will never leave completely behind us—is the perfect symbol of the times. It was a crime without passion, treachery without profit, manipulation and seduction without eros, the great achievement of a people estranged from a sense of themselves. Watergate had to do with effects, with imagery and arrangements for the right lighting on shallow acts performed by men who were too hard either to hate or to love. They were too denatured for that and, as they were drawn to the whirlpool, they became indistinguishable in their blandness, like cuttings from the same plant trembling momentarily on the water's edge before being washed away. Watergate can never be satisfactorily resolved because everything about it—from witnesses to tapes to leading figures—was ambiguous and ill-defined, the accomplishment of people who did wrong in a colorless way, the triumph of a generation that forgot how to sin because it had not truly learned how to live. Martha Mitchell seemed the only passionate character in the long list of those connected with this disembodied affair. It was difficult for preachers—and even editorial writers—to denounce it properly because of the way in which it constantly broke apart in their hands. It is an example of what we come to when we neither love nor sin with much feeling anymore. And that, of course, is why we cannot absolve ourselves or even find out whom to forgive in order to achieve redemption. It all just happened, the accumulation of what occurs when people drift away from themselves, and nobody can clean up the stain it has left on the century. It would be easier to clean if it were a marking in blood; unfortunately, it is faintly odorous protoplasm instead.

We have not had an environment in which we could be authentically bad, and that is not good for human persons. The battle for human liberation is against the blandness that has made effects as much the object of our national life as they seemed to be in the Watergate affair. It does not do, as has been noted, just to condemn these things. It is, however, essential to identify them in order to come to terms with them and to begin to find our way back to ourselves. Make way, the moralist should proclaim, not for the earthly paradise but for a land in which we can be human again.

This is inordinately difficult in a country which, for example, and contrary to the prevailing moral opinion, makes it so difficult for people to commit sexual sins. Genuine sexual sins can only be committed by persons with a feeling for their own identity and an understanding of the violable borders of the personalities of others. It has little to do with the fearful, half-teasing, and generally superficial seductiveness of our culture. It is not that our culture is too sensuous; it simply is not sensuous enough in a powerfully human way. Trifling with erotic effects is not the same as being passionately human. We are, as a people, playing with the edges of sensuousness and settling for disembodied thrills rather than full-bodied or full-blooded sexuality. Sexuality has, unfortunately, entered a long decline from which it will recover only slowly. In the meanwhile we must settle for the kind of diluted eroticism from which we can fashion what we would flatter ourselves to call sins. You have to take sexuality seriously—you have to take yourself seriously —to use it badly or well in life.

This is difficult when the model for our existence is the Watergate person, the bland, well-dressed, efficient team player who gives off no odors and possesses no sharply defined personality. Our national anxiety that we should never give off any smells merely estranges us from our bodies in the same way that we attempt to disengage ourselves from so many of the penalties, as we perceive them, of being human. The new perfectionism idealizes the mechanical person—the Watergate man again—who follows the track toward success in politics, business, and sex in pretty much the same manner. The effect—the image that hypnotizes us out of a concern for substance—is supreme and, as we build this type of world, we find that it is stifling, a choking place because the air is so thin and there seems to be no way out of it. The greatest complaint in our culture is not that people feel free to sin but that they feel trapped in lives in which they are strangers to themselves and to those around them. They do not, in fact, break out very violently; the aggression that arises takes on an aimless and self-directed quality. Life is out there somewhere; there must be more than crabgrass, multiple orgasms, and the need to look as though we had never aged. But where is it? And who will show us the way to begin to take our personalities seriously again?

There is hardly much reason to document the climate that is so familiar to so many persons. It is not that they like or will it to remain the way it is. But they are living in a greenhouse that is getting hotter and more crowded. It is not surprising that so much time and effort go into distracting people from the way their lives are being twisted out of shape. Perhaps it would be better to lead a revolution than to let persons die of the terminal shallowness that affects so many of them. That is why some people turn to revolution; through its ecstasy they recapture a sense of themselves as subjects. Even in desperate conditions this seems a form of redemption unavailable in other circumstances.

Perhaps our cultural difficulty with passion is best attested to by our preoccupation with pornography. It is a sad thing that we have invested so much of our energy and committed our greatest institutions to a phenomenon that is a symptom of our puzzled struggle with life rather than a symbol of our depravity. Nonetheless, both the courts and the Churches are deeply involved with pornography either as the issue that represents our greatest concern about free speech or as the signal of our fundamental option for wickedness. Pornography has little to do with genuine human passion; it flourishes in climates in which persons have been alienated from their feelings, in the wasteland where we find ourselves whenever we get disconnected from our best possibilities as persons. A land filled with pornography may have forgotten to love, and it certainly does not know how to sin. It does know how to distract itself and to keep at a distance from any serious consideration of what the experience of life means. Yet this is unmistakably where we are, a place nobody likes and where nobody is particularly happy but from which we cannot escape as long as our most significant institutions slog in the quicksand of endless discussions and crusades about what is or is not pornographic. An amazing sight indeed! Everybody focused on pornography, while the larger issues of life—its very context, in fact—slips by. America in the seventies: all undressed and no place to go.

Serious persons deserve better than the environment attested to on separate pages of the entertainment newspaper *Variety* for July 3, 1974. On p. 17 we read of the producer's dilemma: how to advertise his latest erotic film to attract the largest audience. The article speaks for itself and puts pornography in better perspective than most court briefs or sermons.

"Score," in trade parlance, is considered a tough sell since it deals with a married couple's seduction of a pair of young marrieds with husband seducing husband and wife ditto wife. Pic has been test dated around the country with three different campaigns, at least two of them avoiding pic's real subject matter. . . . A pitch to straights worked in Weathersfield, Conn., a gay sell didn't work in Los Angeles and a flat-out exploitation "straight" pitch worked in a number of drive-ins and in Atlanta. Problem seems to lie with the straight male sexploitation audience which is turned off by the male-male sex scenes in the pic. Women respond to that footage and the hope is that they will get their escorts to bear with it. . . . New "bi-sexual" campaign is in the works to ride the quest of current liberation, male and female. . . .

On p. 57 we read of a renewed battle in another direction:

Father Morton Hill, S.J., expressed gratification that the Albany legislature had enacted a new obscenity bill for the State of New York. As president of Morality in Media, the priest forecast the new law will "go a long way towards cleaning up Times Square, and stopping the traffic in hardcore pornography from moving into local communities."

Just as the producer's concern is not with the substance of his film but with how he can represent it, truthfully or not, to get customers, so the admirable Father Hill, with the best of intentions, symbolizes the shortsighted and perennially ineffective way that Churches confront the problem of pornography. The argument echoes throughout the decade, and the pornographers go on profiting off a society that has not as yet helped its members to understand the more basic issues about existence that must be faced before pornography can either be understood or sensibly managed. As William F. Buckley noted of the since reversed Supreme

Court decision declaring that pornography should be judged according to "local standards," this could not possibly halt pornography because, lamentably, there exists a notable lack of standards, local or otherwise, about the implications of pornography.

Pornography gives witness to our passionless and depersonalized situation, and it is to the causes of this that the moral attention and energies of our leaders and our institutions can be well directed. The moral pilgrimage of our day requires an ability to understand the elements of our existential dilemma and to acknowledge that we are faced with the profound religious problem of learning to live as human beings. No easy task and not one to be accomplished within our lifetime; it is not like a cure for cancer or some other illness. Life is not a disease we are cured of by seeking a new escape route to perfection through drugs, sex, or emotionalized religion. Life must be accepted on its own badly disorganized and imperfect terms. We have to know the valley through which we are traveling to avoid the impotence of naïve innocence or of jaded cynicism. As long as we distract ourselves or stop short at the symptoms, as we generally do regarding sexual behavior, we will find it almost impossible to get to the moral roots of our existence. We will end up like the narrator of John Cheever's story "The Jewels of the Cabots."[1] Reflecting on his hometown and his travels, he finds himself wanting to come up with happy endings despite the accumulated evidence of human malice and disaster:

Children drown, beautiful women are mangled in automobile accidents, cruise ships founder, and men die lingering deaths in mines and submarines, but you will find none of this in my accounts. In the last chapter the ship comes home

[1] *The World of Apples* (New York: Warner Paperback Library Edition, 1974), pp. 14–34.

to port, the children are saved, the miners will be rescued. Is this an infirmity of the genteel or a conviction that there are discernible moral truths? Mr. X defecated in his wife's top drawer. That is a fact, but I claim that it is not a truth. In describing St. Botolph's I would sooner stay on the West Bank of the river where the houses were white and where the church bells rang, but over the bridge there was the table silver factory, the tenements, and the Commercial Hotel. . . . The telephone rings and the bartender beckons to Doris. There's a customer in room eight. Why would I sooner be on the West Shore where my parents are playing bridge with Mr. and Mrs. Eliot Pinkham in the golden light of a great glass chandelier?

Wandering later in Rome and listening to a wife verbally assault her husband from some nearby apartment, the narrator questions himself once more:

Why would I sooner describe church bells and flocks of swallows? Is this puerile, a sort of greeting-card mentality, a whimsical and effeminate refusal to look at facts? . . . She will go after him with a carving knife and he will end up in the emergency ward of the Policlinico, claiming to have wounded himself, but as I go out for dinner, smiling at beggars, fountains, children and the first stars of evening, I assure myself that everything will work out for the best.

Cheever offers a penetrating exposition of a person journeying on the borders of moral nihilism, buoyed up by an enforced optimism about surfaces and appearances, hoping for happy endings but incapable of facing or involving himself in what such a spiritually bankrupt world might mean. He is a man who wants to believe in good but who is confounded by the complexities of evil and what, if anything, can be done about it. The story is an evocation of the bewilderment of many modern people who make peace

with life through appearances; it is the story of our contemporary malaise. At the same time it is striking that one
of the most confronting and spiritually rich documents
of the age should come from a Russian writer, Solzhenitsyn,
who, through decades of suffering, has found again the
foundation for meaning in life. He has taken existence seriously, his own as well as that of the thousands who went
namelessly to cruel deaths in Russian prisons. He has stared
life in its cold gray eye and has joined himself to do battle
with it. Far more difficult the problem of the affluent Western man and woman who might long for persecution by an
identifiable adversary from whom they might wrest a sense
of spiritual sovereignty once more. They feel dead at the
core, and life is not going to solve their problem for them.
The problem is not their sex life nor their retirement plan;
the problem is life and finding their way back to feeling it
once more.

Who can celebrate life and help people to make their way
across the frozen wasteland once more? It is specifically a
job for the Churches, who possess such vast symbolic resources and traditions that are steeped in the human struggle for meaning. Organized religions lament empty churches
and uninterested youth. And yet one is tempted to think
that if they could marshal even a fraction of their ability
to respond seriously to people—and that is far different
from scolding them or insisting on controlling their behavior—people would take them seriously in return. It is even
true that the Churches have been criticized almost enough;
there are men wise enough within them to know what the
Churches could do if they were willing to risk what they
have acquired in order to speak more directly to the basic
needs of human beings. But that is the problem, isn't it? It
is all so simple in theory and so complex in action, all so
noble to speak of letting go of one's possessions and so seemingly impossible with payrolls to meet, mortgages to pay,

and pensioners to see safely to the grave. But selling the Vatican Museum is not a necessary prelude to the Churches' turning back to the basic crisis in the life of Western man. It takes a kind of passion for life seldom found among Church leaders. Contemporary man is as lost as the prodigal son of the Scriptures, and he desperately needs a religious vision in order to find the right path at the present time. Even if the Churches could identify the problem and withhold their passion from unnecessary fights about things like pornography in order to invest it in liberating persons for life, the effect would be electric.

The issues connected with a restored feeling for existence are not difficult to identify. Religion does not mean indoctrination as much as it suggests the capacity for a sensitive interpretation and symbolization of the human struggle for meaning; it is meant to reinforce a passion for life. Our problems concern the meaning of human personality, the implications of freedom, the implementation of justice, the fight for honesty, the unending battle for human dignity, the great struggle about whether we will possess or be possessed by our advances, the abiding and haunting questions of whether we will find our souls or sell out almost unknowingly for a mess of pottage, of whether we will learn to love or just die passively with all our dreams inside us. We can neither be good nor really very bad until we make more progress in solving the most pressing problem of all, that of reclaiming our identity as human beings. Only then will we regain a passionate moral sense and feel throughout ourselves what it means to be alive. Without that there is nothing left for us in history but hoping for happy endings while our hearts slowly harden against life altogether.

13

A Sense of the Spirit

Fear rather than hate is the great killer of existence; it is fear that takes away life quietly and systematically. Fear also diminishes the possibility of our leading well-developed moral lives. Fear stands opposed to love, the true energy of moral living. Fear deals with our souls like a cowardly mugger, assaulting us and leaving us dazed and bewildered at the side of life.

Fear accomplishes its work in us by turning our concerns to security and the moves that protect us from existence and therefore prevent us from meeting or knowing life very well at all. When we are afraid of loss, we search earnestly for the formula for security. That is one of the basic motivations in undeveloped forms of religion through which people concentrate so much on their own salvation that they close themselves off from their neighbors and from much feeling for the universe itself. We operate out of anxiety when we are so afraid of committing sin that life is considered a temptation to be carefully avoided.

This fear generates obsessiveness—the style, bred by inner

conflict, that keeps us busy but relatively unhappy. People feel that there should be more to life than the uneasy peace that comes from obsessively keeping anxiety at bay, but they are at a loss to discover it. The strategy that delivers security does so at the cost of eliminating risk. Without risk it is difficult to encounter life and it is impossible to be moral in any adult sense. If anything, building one's life on the determination to avoid the risk of failure provides only the beginning of morality. We end up drawing straight lines on which to walk and we never understand the crooked ones with which God writes his wisdom across the universe. Our behavior may be correct, but it is guided more by inner needs than by deliberate choices. It exhibits conformity rather than any profile of our own individual presence in life. Fear takes away our capacity to be present, and so it eliminates our ability to be moral. When we live obsessively, avoiding sin at all costs, we may look good without really being good. Any morality motivated chiefly by fear may be superior to chaos in the streets, but it only suggests the possibilities, it only hints at the strength of the living morality that is shaped by informed personal choices. That emerges in those bold enough to take on life instead of hiding fearfully away from it.

Most of us may be a long way from achieving the kind of full presence in life through which we define our moral sense clearly. We are uneasy about granting ourselves the freedom for such an existence. Yet this is the freedom purchased for us by Jesus, a profound and urgent aspect of God's revelation to us. We work in life at achieving freedom because through this process we are brought closer to understanding the meaning of life. Even some small steps toward affirming life and feeling it surging within ourselves are much better than the anxiety-laden adjustment through which we treat life as though it were a bed of glowing coals either to be avoided or hopped across very swiftly. There is nothing wrong, of course, with not having life all worked out. That is, in fact, one of the conditions of wisdom that surprises but strengthens people at the same time. You do not need to have life all worked out in order to enter into it. Indeed, the fundamental mystery of the Christian revelation comes down to this: to begin the journey of life without being able to see the end of it and to make the journey in faith that overcomes fear.

Assenting to life is not a pagan dream but is rather synonymous with what it means to be a believer. As we begin life, and in a sense we begin it again every day, we encounter the recurrent motifs of the Christian myth, the truths deeper than facts or information, the truths in which we recognize our own truth. The Christian vision has at last been pried loose from time, from a static base in that brief period ended by the death of the last apostle. Nothing was more killing to our sense of life than the notions that all our relevant spiritual history occurred within a few generations around the time of Christ. Jesus told us that the mystery is ever present and so revelation must be a continuing aspect of it; life itself is an invitation to the experience of revelation in and through the complex world of personal relationships. This understanding of Christianity as a continuing living reality rather than a celebration of events that took place a long time ago delivers to us a new historical perspective. Believers neither look back to what happened at Christianity's beginning nor do they rest their faith only on the expectation of what will occur at its ending. Such conceptions of time have no meaning for believers who know that the mystery of living in Christ has neither beginning nor end. It is the now, in this moment and in this day, that life awaits us, displaying its truths and inviting us to understand them in our own lives. Christianity is good news because it is always fresh news; it is a good story because it enables us to recognize our story in its revelation. We find our timeless journey and the experiences that mark it for all of us in the Christian myth. We discover ourselves there and realize that we save ourselves through making the journey of life rather than by avoiding its perils. We know life and achieve adult morality by being on pilgrimage more than by just safely completing the journey. We meet always at the Tree of Eden and the Tree of Calvary, in the mystery of fall-redemption, and in the living experience of death-resurrection. On these themes are organized the days of our lives.

These are the mysteries in which we understand the meaning of our existence, the challenges we cannot side-step, the events through which we discover and deepen our identities and work through and express our morality. Perhaps we need a poet rather than an intellectualized theologian or social scientist in order to find our way through the complications of life. The path can never be etched in frosty statistics or in any single language of theological formulation. The Church as a poet stands free of time, an admirable renegade battling its own institutional hardness of heart through sensing the right direction for a sacramental existence. Jesus led this kind of poetic life himself. He was not, after all, a member of the clergy of his day nor did he allow himself to be absorbed by the institutional religion whose pillars he came to shake. He came to stand against time as the Alpha and the Omega, the man who said "Before Abraham came to be, I am." Nor did Jesus emphasize literal actions or statements but rather underscored the abiding constants, the purifying mysteries of everyday life experience.

Our morality emerges from our willingness to feel these same rhythms in our own lives and to assent to them, to affirm our incarnation, and so to enter the kingdom of the Spirit. The journey to adult morality can never be made merely by training people to perform certain external actions. The process of internalizing the motivations for moral behavior involves our inner selves. Such a journey is made from the inside out. Developed morality flows from an inhabited life, and may be observed in the existence of those who face and deal with the many-layered difficulties involved in being alive. Morality imposed under the pressure of external control collapses quickly when supervision is absent. This is not the morality that people can identify as their own because it is grounded in fear rather than in the substance of authentic inner discovery.

The first mystery for the Christian and the continuing mystery for all of us centers on the meaning of incarnation, the central reality of the Christian revelation. Incarnation is indeed so central that some people have not been able to notice it. They have looked for something more complicated. Incarnation has become something to argue about theologically, so that the mystery has been shredded by the litter of fine points that have obscured its thundering message. Being alive, taking on the flesh of this unforgiving human situation, and keeping each other alive through the gift of resurrection: These are the broad dimensions of Christian existence. That is what God told us by becoming a man. Each of us begins the journey anew, and each of us must make it for ourselves. By any estimation it is a hazardous trip, and the contradictions outnumber the consistencies all along the way. It is complex to become a person and, in the course of life, to taste the mysteries through which we begin to understand who we are. The meaning of our lives—obscure as that may be to us at any one point during them—derives from the fact that we express our relationship to God through our incarnational experience. The temptation has always been to try to find some other way in which to live with God. People have always looked for ways to save themselves from mistakes and to preserve themselves from the imperfections that are so much a part of ordinary living. These voyages, whether out into the desert or into some utopian commune, have been variously described, but they are always motivated by a fear and dislike of the world and the bubbling ambivalence of life itself.

Better then to turn away from the place where the deadly sins live, where we have the power to kill each other, and where we settle for second- and third-best adjustments to lessen the pain of existence. Life is a difficult place because the hopeful can become burned-out cases, the lively can grow ill, old, and mean, and we taste the joy of love and friendship at the price of also knowing the hell of loneliness and abandonment. Life is the place where everything happens and so little seems to work out or to make any sense. In life we find that the wicked prosper, the innocent suffer, and separation and struggle seem to be built into each day even for people who love each other very much. In such a life the mysteries are revealed to and by those who have said *yes* to their own incarnation. This is not always the action of the wise and the learned. The perennial gift to the pure of heart is that they can indeed see God. Thus Harvard professor Rudolf Arnagim recently described such an experience. "Not long ago in Grand Central Station I noticed an elderly woman lugging a suitcase. 'Heavy, isn't it?' I said. And she, with an Old World accent, 'The whole life is heavy!' "[1] That is a sample of revelation in everyday life, the art and poetry of redemption.

Life is not only heavy but it is also noisy, ill-ordered, and seemingly more unjust than just. But none of it, neither the broken promises nor the broken hearts, can be escaped by trying to live with God alone. God's invitation is not that we live just with him. It is far more complex, fine and mysterious as a spider web, and it takes a lifetime to begin

[1] New York *Times* (July 13, 1974), p. 23.

to understand it. God asks us rather to live with each other and through this to discover what it means to live in and through him. It is not an easy thing, Boris Pasternak once wrote, to live life to the end. The fundamental Christian invitation is to start living it, to open ourselves to the Spirit, and to make the journey with the kind of love that is only found on imperfect pilgrimages, the kind of love that matches and expresses our human truth and delivers an increasing fraction of insight into God at the same time.

Life is lived on the edge of a cosmic geological fault, and the ground rumbles under our feet all the time. But that is where the Tree of Eden and the Tree of Calvary are planted. Their shadows fall across our lives to remind us of the contradictions that accompany the discovery of our own freedom as well as the dark and awesome mystery of defining our lives through our own choices. Nobody lives happily ever after. We live happily when we live with a sense of purpose and when we are unafraid of living in a world in which things are seldom settled, few things are permanently improved, and where love does not take care of itself. We constantly come up against things we would rather not feel or think about. That is what life delivers to us all the time, the repeated awkward choices through which we chart our moral positions. We struggle to understand what we believe in and what we live by, and we are constantly challenged to re-examine our position in the light of an ever deeper experience of the Christian mysteries.

No, it is not simple, and we feel its pain when we are confronted, for example, by a public discussion on an issue like abortion. It is so difficult to try to approach the truth and to take a position that represents our own convictions when people are shouting at us from both sides. When power is exerted even in defense of the position in which we believe we are made uneasy and sometimes unsure about ourselves. We would like somebody else to solve it or think about it for us. We will believe what people tell us, and we would just as soon leave the reasoning to the theologians; say *yes* or *no* and move back into the quiet again. And yet life is the issue at the heart of the discussion about abortion. That is true of all the significant issues, such as the meaning of personality, the values we attach to existence, and the conditions that are vital for a full human life for all persons. Our whole view of the human experience is tied up in almost any central focusing question. We can feel the effects of the fall as we face or want to look away from these complicated issues. We can feel that fall in the arguments and disagreements, in the estrangements that are unwilled, in the anger that comes from unconscious sources and the loneliness that we do not want but that we sometimes seem to make for ourselves all the time. In the midst of this boiling sea of existence we are invited, not to look the other way, but to involve ourselves with understanding. In the center of such difficulties we are given the power to heal each other and to redeem each other as a daily gift of concern and love. We are moral when we accept the invitation because we understand that we work out our salvation in and through accepting what can seem to be a tragic existence. It is only tragic in that we can make only a segment of the journey toward solving these problems more adequately.

Friendship and love are the prime examples of the experiences in which we discover both the wonder and the pain of life and through which we construct our moral selves. They are compelling experiences of revelation in which we face death and resurrection continually. We can grow tired of such hurts and we can give up on love. Nor is it surprising that we want to hide away or draw within ourselves or simply put an end to life, which seems to be an environment of shattered glass for so many persons. Death and resurrection are the double daily experience of Christians who know that religion is not concerned only with old truths but also with the timeless truths we taste all the time. That, indeed, is why authentic faith stands outside of time. It is the reality, the spiritual environment in which we all meet, without beginning or end, the mystery that enfolds our lives through which we establish our moral presence and make purchase of meaning.

In the perspective of these conditions for being alive, other recurrent themes of the New Testament begin to make sense for us. We can understand, for example, why there is so much insistence on the fact that there is no law for a person who truly lives by the Spirit. Laws have no meaning anymore for persons living by the Spirit. St. John of the Cross wrote on the mount of perfection that there was no road leading there. We find our own way freely and by ourselves. So too life cannot be described or summed up in laws that may make us feel secure by identifying for us what is or is not the right thing. Our morality is defined not in following regulations, not by trapping the Spirit through our rules, but by breaking loose from the burden of external law through taking responsibility for our own existence. The Incarnation asks us to take our lives seriously and, living by the Spirit, we are freed from the laws that diminish our participation or control of our own existence.

It is clear that God sent his only-begotten son to tell us that it is life that counts and that entering into its multiple contradictions permits us to understand and overcome our sinfulness. It is not surprising, as we read the Gospels, to discover that Jesus is always found with the least likely people, with the outcasts and sinners rather than with the self-righteous and those who are sure that they have discovered a secure way to please God. Jesus came to tell us that his kingdom is one for sinners, for people who take risks in life and who regularly fall but who are nonetheless called ahead of the just to come close to him.

There is an immense but simple secret involved in the

way Jesus lived so close to people like ourselves. We live close to him whenever we are as unafraid of our own humanity as he was. The sin against the Spirit is that through which we reject life, interpret it in absolute but deadened terms, or make it impossible for others to experience it in any deep and free manner. Jesus came to tear the curtains of hypocrisy away from the front of the Temple, to proclaim that the altar was made for man, not the other way around, and to give us the gift of the Spirit to guide us along the rutted path of existence, where we both test and express our morality.

14

A Sense of Wholeness

What delivers a sense of wholeness to a human being? When and in what circumstances do we feel that we live with integrity and that our behavior reflects the generous commitment to fairness and love that gives a fullness to our actions, a sense that we give what we can without hedging, undue distortion, or faking? A sense of wholeness means that we feel right about the way they live. This is not the same as the outcome of the invitation to indulge ourselves and to feel good because we have allowed ourselves to feel everything. Neither is it the result of the pills distributed by various Drs. "Feelgood" who believe that a drug-induced nirvana is just as good as the satisfaction that flows from living truly. There is no other way to wholeness and to the peace that it brings except through living open-handedly, honestly, with a willingness to accept if not seek out suffering, and a steady effort to live for something besides ourselves. That is what gives the finished quality to a person's life; that is why some persons who die young project a completeness even though others weep at what they might yet accomplish. Such people are already whole, and they come to death neither incomplete nor unfulfilled.

A sense of wholeness is not the same as merely escaping anxiety. Some people spend large amounts of energy attempting to forestall or avoid the experience of anxiety. This is the classic neurotic game through which individuals develop various symptomatic styles to fend off the ravages of worry. This is not, of course, a wholly conscious choice on the part of the neurotic. Such a solution deceives us because it sidesteps rather than solves our basic psychological conflict. Such anguished psychological footwork offers us an example of those who feel that a sense of moral wholeness can be achieved by covering all life's possible moves, by seeing that they have met all the stated requirements for religious and moral integrity. They struggle uncomfortably to avoid the anxiety of living more openly; they try to block out the risks of living to stake a shaky claim on some sense of security.

This is as old as the Gospel story of the man who pointed with satisfaction to the barns he had filled with grain for the winter without knowing that he was going to die that night. A sense of wholeness is not, however, the same as a sense of security, nor is it related to the immature religious notion that if we save ourselves, we are home free. That attitude, unfortunately, allows us to stay on the outside of life by choosing and carrying through the moves that make it impossible for anyone to accuse us of serious fault. That is what Pilate did by washing his hands of the blood of Jesus. It is like the statement once made to me by a churchman who described how he had carefully issued the warnings dictated by canon law in trying to keep one of his priests from asking for permission to leave the priesthood. He had done everything to the letter, but he did not face the man's conflict with him nor face the conflict in himself caused by this man's decision to leave the active ministry. He turned to me after the last proper warning had been issued and said, "Now no one can accuse me of not having done everything that I could in trying to help this man." He felt secure, but he was not whole.

Covering all the bases is not the same as living with the integrity that is less careful but is honest and true as it flowers from a commitment to a full, honest, and human life. Just as neurotic symptom formation gives us a spurious sense of satisfaction, so too do the general approaches to morality that make us feel secure from accusation because we have kept ourselves at a great distance from genuine involvement in crucial human situations. Whenever we say, "I have done everything" or "I am covered" or "I said my prayers," we sound faintly like the man in the Temple counting off his virtues to make sure that the Lord God was aware of them and of him. A moral life does not depend so much on having every answer—its secret is not in the art of the trial lawyer—nor on covering every conceivable possibility. A sense of wholeness does not derive from having the political response that makes us look good or that works pragmatically in certain situations. These may be widespread maneuvers, and they may, in fact, be generally understandable as reflections of personal struggle at an intermediate level of moral development. But persons interested in the meaning of integrity in their own lives cannot content themselves with such self-protecting strategies.

Such broken-field running constitutes a major effort to avoid shame rather than to deal with the meaning of guilt. Shame, if anything, is, as a wise psychiatrist once stated, "a primitive precursor of guilt." The high point of this powerful and strongly motivating force has been reached in the age of what social critics David Riesman and Eric Fromm have called the "outer directed" person. Our recent history has shown the lack of substance in the pseudomorality that is generated when the strongest motive for behavior is the avoidance of shame. Like a plant without roots, it can only straggle along the ground, totally dependent on a balance of outer conditions for survival. Rootless people who depend on the messages of their environment for their moral positions have no inner source of nourishment or stability if there is a sharp change in the weather. Shame works, but it builds a world in which "waffling," that peculiar contemporary flip-flopping on moral positions, is the maneuver of survival. Shame is extremely functional, but when its weakness is exposed as a motivating force, when looking good and covering all the bases no longer suffice, its immaturity as the determiner of moral action is obvious. When all that works is shame, there is not much to us as moral persons.

The "inner directed" person, on the other hand, attempts to discover and understand the reality of guilt as an experience that is appropriate in an honest life. Such persons ask much of themselves and are constantly concerned about where and how their shadows fall across those around them. It is extremely difficult to lead a developed moral life because of the continuing and exacting demands it makes on our self-awareness and concern. It is much easier to stay at the level of avoiding punishment by doing what we are told and waffling our way through things. The saddest thing about the handsome Jeb Stuart Magruder's Watergate reflections is his apparent failure to realize that these are internal principles of moral behavior. There is little evidence in his book that an inner source of morality ever even dawned on him as a possibility.

Indeed, why go deeper into the self? Why care, especially in this age when we are told that the former persuasions of religious faith no longer possess their once strong imperative force for us? Why look into one's self when we are no longer scared to death by the eternal punishment of the brightly burning hellfires that torture but never consume condemned sinners, when we have reached the point in history when the myths of heaven and hell, as they were once understood in a rather primitive and elementary way, no longer bind us to strict external moral codes? Were we cured of our obsessiveness, would we be moral at all? The cynic wonders whether we should be so concerned about self-examination when even a casual inspection of the world says that the powerful and corrupt continue to be rewarded while the innocent and undefended suffer more grievously than ever before. What purpose the good life when it seems to avail so little here and no longer to promise so much hereafter? What reason can we find outside of ourselves for moral concern in what some observers describe as the wreckage of the Christian view of life?

Where does this leave the believer? Do we stand in need of some new form of religion to embolden us to face the darkness all around? Many thoughtful persons, surveying the moral chaos of the times, seem to feel that this is the case. Literature, according to critic Irving Howe, is charged now with a "search for a moral style . . . that may save us after the collapse of our myths." This search for anchor points on the part of poets and artists "almost demands that it provide us with norms of value we cannot find in our experience."[1]

Can art find a way if the force of religion is no longer effective in informing us about our moral sense of direction? It is a profound question, which confronts us with the seriousness of the issues that are involved. Is religion bankrupt? This is a fundamental issue because, if faith no longer provides a vision of meaning for existence, then the scramble for new and usable interpretations of life may be hectic but unpromising. It is possible, although not entirely fashionable, to say that we do not stand at the edge of the precipice. We are not at the end of the age of religious awareness. We

---

[1] "Literature of the Latecomers: A View of the Twenties," *Saturday Review/World* (August 10, 1974), p. 43.

stand rather in the foothills of the self, at the beginning of
an understanding of what authentic religion can and should
mean in helping us to discover our true wholeness as persons.
We are not on the edge of nothingness but rather in a place
where we can at last begin to see everything. Having put
aside magic, manipulative external controls, and other forces
of shame that have made it so difficult to understand even
the beginnings of guilt, we are at the doors of the kingdom
within us. We begin to survey the incredible and intertwined strands of our complex but authentic human
identity. But this deep and extensive territory of the ego is
as yet little explored. Still, it is the soil in which a more developed religious awareness can take root and grow. It is
into this strange and misty place deep within our personalities where flow still the dreams of our ancestors. Here we
can hear the clear throbbing of our unconscious selves; this
is, in fact, our homeland. *Homo religiosus* is not the outer-
directed person but the individual who, having seemed to
lose the supports of external religion, has at last found the
way to the riches of humanity from which one can shape a
lasting sense of wholeness. We have died to something
primitive in religion and awakened to its truth in our own
truth.

It is in our true selves—and it is no easy task even to look
at, much less assemble an authentic picture of ourselves—
that we can believe again. The Gospels are not just about
wonders outside of us, not about lightning bolts or revenge
for actions committed unknowingly. They center rather on
love and on the proper use of ourselves in our lives with each
other. Here, inside of ourselves, we begin to forge our own
moral shield. That it is invisible makes it no less real. It
coexists with our vulnerability, and so it is something that
comes out of us rather than covers us over. A moral sense
does not merely protect us from life but also actually grows
out of the interplay of our real selves with our own world. A

moral style is the product of our purposeful interactions not only with our true selves but also with the true selves of those with whom we share life. This inner kingdom of the self is not a hide-a-way where we shut out the world. It is the point at which we become enough of ourselves to be able to enter into the world with a new and more refined perception because our identity is more secure and more wonderful than an oversimplified view of life led us to expect. The mystery of incarnation unfolds here, inviting us to discover our still unsuspected strengths, the kingdom within, where the Spirit broods. It is an almost timeless place, for we carry some inheritance of all who have lived as well as possibilities in our psychophysiological structure that we have not touched. We touch the still trembling roots of God's creation in ourselves.

The purpose of religion is to declare this revelation to us, to enlarge its vision every day, and to celebrate its mysteries through living rituals and symbols. Religion is not meant to distract us from finding out who we are, nor is it meant to forbid us to gaze into our own experience. Religion's aim is to end our estrangement from our own experience, from the sense of our unique passage through and understanding of life. We no longer live in the howling void where we had to take the words of others or find magic stones and amulets in order to secure our journey. The challenge is now far deeper, because we have to travel to the deepest part of ourselves to know our existence. Our identity is realized as we find the words for that experience of ourselves. The Christian task is to make the world of the self into flesh, to give birth to one's authenticity from within.

We all feel these groanings within ourselves. They are as deep and rumbling as those that St. Paul heard in the universe itself. These are the true cries for fulfillment that we cannot stifle without slowly killing ourselves. Toward this sense of self some people stumble blindly. They know that they are in pain, that they are missing something, but they cannot find anything to make sense of their inner experience. It is this experience, this core of the self, that is the subject of Christianity. Strip Christianity of everything else and it remains built on the notion of our becoming persons and sharing life in the richness of our experience together. Literature joins in the search for a moral stance and attempts to uncover for us what we fear our former religious awareness could never deliver. Wholeness comes from assenting to life, from trusting the impulses of the Spirit that allow us to grapple slowly but successfully with the question of our identity. A richer wholeness comes as we commit ourselves to this long unfolding of our incarnation. Making the transfer from outer-directedness to inner-directedness constitutes our achievement of our own moral style.

The fact that this is enormously difficult, that many people struggle under great obstacles and still fail to achieve a satisfactory sense of themselves—none of these things can discourage us. In Christianity it is always the journey, rather than the completion of it, that counts. It has always been a faith of pilgrimages. How do we make the journey? What questions do we ask to find out if we are even on the right road? Most of us do not want to look too steadily at ourselves. We have become too conditioned to shame and its punishing effects to want to discover the fullness of who we are. Many people are, in fact, discouraged about their own existence. They feel that they do not measure up and that they could never measure up if their true identities were exposed to the view of others. The great source of encouragement to all persons lies in the Christian invitation to take heart. This compassionate theme echoes throughout the Gospels, which are a pressing invitation to the poor, the lame, and the imperfect to discover the real sources of life within themselves. We need not fear nor need we worry about the shame that seems to put us off or to control so much of our behavior. We may have to treat ourselves with understanding and with a certain amount of gentleness, but these are not incompatible with facing the truth about our own existence. Wholeness comes when we look toward the truth that bellies out in the uncharted darkness of the ego. That is where we live.

The question, then, comes down in practice to asking how we can take ourselves seriously as human beings. We must discover, not through some trickery or glib self-reassurance, whether and how fully we have been alive during each day. We come back to ask how present we are in life: How much of us is really there, either for ourselves or for others? It is very easy to build our day on dodging inconveniences and in getting by with minimal involvement with other persons. One can do this out of fear or out of immaturity. Sometimes people do this because they have such a diminished idea of themselves. Their whole sense of personality has been based on the way others react to them, and so the discovery of their true selves—or even that they have a right to recognize their true selves—is long delayed. There is something more, they know, but it seems so difficult to get it in view.

It is important for persons to ask whether they think it is significant to cast light on their own behavior. A modern examination of conscience is one that centers on our total personalities. Only from the fullness of ourselves do any actions with any measure of wholeness about them arise. To know whether we are moral or not, in other words, it is not enough to ask what we think about or what we speak about. We have to catch ourselves, as a candid photographer might, in an unself-conscious moment that reveals the truth of ourselves as whole persons.

This may begin by inspecting what we think about. Thoughts alone, however, never killed anybody, and the long game that has made people think that their moral life consisted in strenuously controlling their thoughts is one of the factors that gave rise to the Catholic conflict of obsessiveness. Morality that creates neurotic conflicts has something wrong with it because it prevents persons from taking a full look at themselves. Perhaps the biggest problem connected with this is that we have presumed for so long that morality is a logical business. It is anything but that. We do not understand our moral selves by trying to put our thoughts into ethical syllogisms. That is not the way we operate. We need a new sense of ourselves and of the magic and mystery of our existence that we only begin to grasp as we stand at the foothills of our true personalities. We are still out there, like unvisited lands, awaiting discovery.

It takes a while to learn the language that we speak to ourselves, the language of morality through which our true personalities are expressed. This is the same language that we speak to others. Through this tongue we make ourselves present to God as well as to each other. If we do not understand it, we will never find our true selves, nor will we be able to deal adequately or sensitively with the meaning of guilt in our lives. We will always be on the outside of ourselves, trying to impose logic and only being frustrated by the task. We can only understand and grow to take possession and responsibility for ourselves when we understand this human language that comes from our depths. It is illogical, but it is profoundly and freshly human. We find ourselves and the key to our inner pilgrimage in that language.

In a real sense we have to overhear ourselves. We must see ourselves from the corner of our eyes rather than by looking directly down into our brains. We must watch our behavior from the outside, catching a glimpse of the unretouched truth, as we sometimes do when we see our image suddenly reflected in a store window. We need to stand back and see the shape of our lives. There are many subtle indicators that indirectly deliver a sense of who we really are. What, for example, gets done first every day? And what gets done last? If we have to change our plans, whose plans do we change? We learn a lot about ourselves just by finding out who the people are in our lives that we are willing to inconvenience. If we think about it for a while, we realize that when we have to cancel something, we usually do it in a characteristic way, and often to the same person. We let someone else bear the burden for us. Who is it in our lives, anyway? And why should it be this person? This is only one line of inquiry, but such indirect hints help us to overhear ourselves and to see ourselves as the candid photographer might.

How do we spend our time? Is time a factor in our lives? What makes us uncomfortable? What are the things that we try to avoid? If we were fairly to graph the direction of our journey in life, what would the resulting black line tell us? It might indicate that we seldom meet anything head on or that we seek out only those situations in which no other people are going to applaud or like us very much. Life may reveal itself as a long series of self-contained maneuvers, defensive postures carefully assumed that prevent other people from getting too close. Our moral character is revealed far more in this continuous graph than in any single thought or action. We stand revealed in the undulating line that shows the direction of our days. That movement is made by us, and it tells the story of what we are about and what we think is significant to accomplish during each day. This dark and sloping line is a source of revelation, blinding as it lights up the territory in which we discover just what we do both to ourselves and to others in everyday life.

We might examine the chart of our activities closely to find out if there is any consistency or continuity in what we do or in how we spend our time. We might even discover something about what we do all day long and whether it has any enlarging effects on the lives of those close to us. Here, indeed, we discover something that reveals clearly our moral stature. How do I see others in my life? Or do I see them at all? It is sometimes possible for us to consider others only insofar as they provide rewards of one kind or another to us. Sometimes other persons are threatening, and we find good reasons to avoid them. It is also possible for us to view other persons as transients, those who come and go but at whose faces we hardly look and whose concerns are not important enough for us to notice.

Suppose we travel deeper into some of the familiar regions of our self-experience that for so long have been almost the sole concern of moral theologians. This is the area of our feelings. These are major dimensions of personality from which the refractions of our true identity can easily be seen. We might once have been terribly concerned about sins connected with, for example, feelings of anger or sexuality. These feelings seemed once to have a life of their own, the existence of enemies outside of us. This is no time to raise issues about the former controlling and suppressing nature of Church attitudes toward these human experiences. It is clear, however, that the heavy oppression that estranged people from a true sense of their feelings also contributed to the awkwardness with which sexuality and anger are still dealt with in the world today. There is no question that the subject of sex needs cooling in our culture; many persons with an external code of morality would be amazed to learn how their determination to suppress it only keeps it heated up.

Personally, we can do much to free ourselves from the oppression of the past narrow vision of these issues by seeing them in the context of our over-all personalities. How, indeed, do I inhabit such feelings? Perhaps we can understand such emotions better if we discover what the focusing point of our sexuality is. We might begin to wonder what we say to ourselves and to others through the special language of our sexuality. Our moral style is revealed in our answer to this question. What do I do as a person who is capable of sexual or strong feelings? What am I like as a sexual person; what is its meaning as part of me? Do I ever even try to find out? Or does sexuality seem a separate aspect of life rather than something that is essentially me? Do I own my sexuality or my anger? Or do I disown and stand away from these elements of personality? To ask these questions and to follow them through, sketching the pattern of our answers plunges us into the mystery of our own revelation. The graph would reveal our sense of purpose as human beings and tell us whether we reach out to others or only draw others selfishly toward ourselves. We might even discover the level we live at and how much of us is present there at any moment. It would all be there, easy to find and convincing in its clarity about our moral style. We would be there facing ourselves, surprised perhaps at what we are like in clear light.

Some people feel that to pursue these questions would make them fall apart. In fact, even asking such questions begins to draw us together in the true experience of our wholeness. There is nothing within us we have to fear. We should, however, be deeply concerned if we do not know in what direction we are moving or if we are largely unaware of the true shape of our lives. Asking the right questions contributes to our sense of wholeness because it involves us in making flesh of the word of our personal truth. The moral person rests everything on that truth, which is at once the source of healing and of growth. We are never fully healed in the human situation; we all continue to process ourselves in relationship to other persons for as long as we live. The Christian mystery is our homeland in this kind of life. It cannot proceed unless we are ready to lose a lot of our self-concern in the death that precedes any awareness of what it means to come alive in Christ through loving each other. But that is where we live as total human persons; in finding out how we deal with and use ourselves in life, we understand and define our personal morality. That is where it stands; that is what our lives mean. We write our signatures across our existence with all of rather than just a part of ourselves.

What is the center of gravity for my life as a person? Do I hurt others as a seeker of revenge, as an evener of old scores? Do I try to reach others for their sake, forgiving both them and myself for all the mistakes that are made along the way? Do I think about or even seem to have a purpose that I have worked through for myself? Or do I still accept my morality as something externally packaged for me, a substance separate from me that I can neither inspect nor question? If I were to write a description of what my life means, what would it sound like right now? These are not meant to be frightening questions. They are the inquiries we make when we are genuinely concerned about our moral lives. There is no other way we can make purchase of a sense of our wholeness.

The sense of our wholeness follows our sense of purpose. This does not exclude mistakes. It allows us, if anything, to see our sins as they truly are. It enables us to feel guilty when that is precisely what we should feel for having offended others, for having failed ourselves, for having experienced the negative side of who we are and how we operate. We live always with the possibility of sin; honesty about it should neither surprise nor discourage us. Sin is easy to forgive; God has told us that many times. It is not, therefore, in avoiding sin completely that we forge a moral life; it is in risking ourselves in some commitment to an always fuller and more loving life that we find the sense of wholeness that delivers peace to us.

We will never be complete as persons. Most of us may

spend our lives just at the beginning of getting the pieces of ourselves together. Our moral lives are a continuing achievement built on an increasing awareness of ourselves and on the meaning and effects of our activities. That we only glimpse part of our journey or that we only make a few inches of progress in our lifetime means that we succeed rather than fail. Making the journey, the commitment to the deep, inexhaustible, and sometimes frightening truth about ourselves—these are the essential ingredients. An expanding fraction of wholeness is enough to define our pilgrimage. Individuals who live like this possess the Spirit, who places them beyond the category of laws. This does not put them in opposition to law. It means that in their fullness and in their freedom they have found the life in which law no longer has a meaning for them. They now live from within, cleansed and refreshed by the waters rising to eternal life, and wholeness is their prize.

15

Common Sense

In the long run, that familiar but still elusive quality we call common sense governs our moral lives. It allows us to put aside the many ways we put up a good front and thereby deny access to our personalities even to ourselves. There is something down to earth about common sense, something that reminds us that the root for the word humility is found in the Latin word for earth. Humility, not much of a virtue when, as Norman Mailer has said, ego is the word of the century. Yet it is the first ingredient of common sense because it makes us face ourselves, not as penitential saints with ash-stained knees restlessly proclaiming our lack of virtue under our mantle of sackcloth, but just as we are in the human situation. Humility is not a virtue of denial; it is one of celebration because it underscores the truth of our lives.

Humility is not difficult because it makes us register false claims about hypothetical wickedness but because it bids us to appraise the elements of our personalities as existential creations shaped like those of no one else. Humility means common sense about ourselves as unique subjects in life. It allows us to cross-section our egos and to see and feel more than the surface awareness of our presence in life. We begin to sense dimensions of ourselves that we may hardly have acknowledged in a full-bodied way previously. Sometimes it is as difficult to recognize and act on our possibilities for good as it is to face our potential for bad. The virtue of common sense tells us that somewhere in the balance between ourselves and others, in that existential field of achieved awareness about our needs and theirs, we discover our moral style.

Our moral style is not a set of principles that stand outside of us as static and dead reference points. It is rather the way we are in action, and it depends on our understanding of ourselves in some depth. Only an accurate awareness of our identity informs our actions with humanity and stamps them with our individual seal. Through this we perceive the operational meaning of the moral life as our continuing effort to become loving persons. Such a vision of morality is neither sentimental nor soft. Learning to love in an adult manner includes the pursuit of justice and a clear recognition of the rights of others. It demands also that we deal with our psychological conflicts and quirks, those shaded areas of our personalities that can so easily make us the victims of motives that we do not understand.

Some people go through life defending a distorted image of themselves in the classic trap of undeveloped unawareness. As a result they find it difficult to impress their own moral mark on their lives. Not understanding their own inner language, they feel estranged from the sources of their own choices. This limitation of responsibility not only weakens their moral style but also leaves them with the dull-edged frustration that is the most poisonous consequence of failed self-knowledge. They do not know the truth about their own good and evil, and so they pass through life without ever knowing quite what happened to them. Life and moral style depend on an ever surer hold on understanding who we are.

Morality, of course, does not consist in never doing anything wrong, although this notion has been presented over the ages in countless visions and revisions of the perfectible person. The virtuous life has been guaranteed in a variety of ways, from the detailed prescriptions of religious order rules to the simple discipline of commune life. But the crack in the column of personality will not be covered over. Morality by rule belongs to the same family of obsessive approaches that attempts to deliver security in living. Compliant external behavior certainly beats chaos, but it partakes only of the rudiments of morality. Indeed, the Catholic conflict described earlier is clearly related to the search to get life right, to guarantee inner serenity through outer propriety.

Our moral style does not depend solely on understanding how to overcome sin totally nor to put it aside completely. This does not mean that we have to be defeated by evil; it means that we have to be realistic about it. That means that we have to look ourselves in the eye, common-sense fashion, and recognize evil as a possibility, as an abiding part of ourselves that cannot be controlled by rules. Evil is not an oppression from without, not a temptation by imagined foes or betraying spirits all around us. Evil is something we can do. Unless we sense something of our power to do wrong, we cannot perceive the moral meaning of our lives at all. There is something essentially moral in facing and coming to terms with our own capacity for sin. It is never far away anyway. We do not handle it well by boarding up certain aspects of our personality and projecting evil out onto fantasied creatures of the night outside of us. The talent for wrongdoing is our own, deeply rooted in us, and it will not easily be disowned.

We do not have to become friendly with sin in order to

live with it. We do, however, have to become keenly aware
of ourselves as potential sinners. There are consequences
to our actions; our prime moral responsibility lies in understanding how we define ourselves morally through the
choices we make. And we see more clearly in their effects on
us and others. To identify evil as something distant from us
may be an understandable psychological mechanism. It has
generated devils and other moral escape devices throughout
the centuries. But we cannot look away from the evil in us
without losing perspective on the rest of ourselves. Part of
our modern alienation arises from failing to have an adequate common-sense picture of ourselves.

What place have the Commandments and rules? It is not
negligible, even though essential morality is rooted in deep
living. The Commandments are an attempt to put into words
some of our hard-bought wisdom about our power for good
and evil. The meaning of the rule is not in the letter but in
the kind of truth it attempts to capture. Observing the letter
of the law for its own sake has always killed people. The
Commandments are a way we have of trying to talk about
our complex human experience. Along with laws and regulations, they constitute yet another special language for us to
understand if we are going to appreciate their meaning in
our lives.

The language of law is as imperfect as any, although it has
occasionally suffered delusions of grandeur. That does not
invalidate the attempt to describe guidelines for human behavior. It does not bankrupt the wise person's efforts to offer
a sense of direction to those still learning about life. The
Commandments are significant because of what they sym-
bolize about human experience. They take on their meaning
from life; life does not take on its meaning from the Commandments. It is impossible to find our way inside of life if
you begin by strictly following laws that never permit us to
experiment or to discover the varied aspects of personality

—including good and evil—that constitute ourselves. We can, however, understand the law much better if we enter into life in a sufficiently deep way. We can appreciate and accept the law with its virtues and its limitations once we have struggled with the substance of life for ourselves. We can see the imperfect wisdom of law and respect it without allowing it to dominate our lives.

This is a far more complicated task than some persons suppose. It is not enough just to do away with law. That perennial romantic temptation is not common sense at all. When St. Paul speaks about certain people reaching a state in which the law no longer has meaning for them, he refers to those who have attained considerable moral awareness and maturity. These people have faced themselves and have developed the capacity to make their own choices from within. Their decisions do not contradict sensible laws, but neither do they depend on them. Persons who live from within themselves are not anxious to banish law. It is simply not something that bothers their lives. They do not find it oppressive because they no longer have to take it into account; they understand that laws do not fit every situation and that an awareness of the complexity of each moral challenge slightly alters the shape of their personal responses. Their sense of direction corresponds to the generalized awareness that is made concrete in good commandments and regulations. Good laws are built on an understanding of human personality, and they neither contradict nor distort it.

Forgiveness is sometimes thought of as a species of softheartedness, something almost too gentle to be involved with the power of evil. But forgiveness is neither softhearted nor softheaded; it is tough and unblinkingly realistic when it is rooted in an accurate understanding of what can go on between us and others. An old tradition of Christianity says that forgiveness begins in forgiving ourselves. This is closely

related to the common-sense humility through which we perceive our truth and live by and through it. That is a necessary condition for identifying and accepting the fact that
we can do things to hurt ourselves and others. Forgiveness is
not something that looks away as though nothing has ever
happened. Far sturdier than that, it sees clearly the results
of our choices. We cannot adequately or justly accuse or
forgive ourselves unless we know honestly what we have
done. Neurotic guilt flares only when we do not really understand ourselves. Real guilt, the kind associated with a
decision to hurt or deceive or betray, can only be handled
by the equally strong medicine of forgiveness.

Forgiveness is in itself a moral activity. Through it we
reach out to ourselves and to others in a balanced way, acknowledging the wound with a loving readiness to heal it.
All healing needs air; it cannot take place in the dark, and
wounds that are closed before they are cleaned out only become more dangerous. Forgiveness is something that draws
us toward the light and into the fresh air. Redemption is
the name we give to the experience of working through our
mutual need for forgiveness. Redemptive forgiveness depends on honesty, and just speaking the truth to each other
is enough to begin the healing process. This does not mean
that there will be no scar. The scar, in fact, will be the sign
that a powerful and effective moral exchange has taken
place.

The first problem is to identify the infection correctly.
What is it we suffer from? Many people do not want to look
that closely at themselves because they are made uneasy
by such self-examination, even though, at some other level,
they long for it. They would like to get at the heart of things,
but they do not know how they can do this or in whose
presence it would ever be safe to do it. They desire a clear
view of themselves and an honest appraisal of their choices
and their responsibility for them. It is dark where we must

journey into ourselves to understand something about the power to sin, with which we must live all our lives. Forgiveness follows as we begin this journey. It is as long and difficult as all the important things connected with the human situation, but it is a common-sense trip at that. Without a sense of sin, without a sense of how we can shed blood, there can be no forgiveness.

It is obviously true that people suffering from psychological difficulties are hindered from understanding themselves and from either sinning seriously and, at times, even loving deeply. One can only recognize that it is a difficult thing to sin. Sin is a power unleashed consciously and directly rather than the outcome of carelessness or forgetfulness. Such sloppy thinking about sin—as in identifying it with neurosis —has kept us from taking its measure more accurately. It has also encouraged us to view it in a depersonalized way, as though it were an entity outside ourselves. Real sin is an achievement made colder and more deadly by the fact that we do it; it is our product. Nor is it easy to be moral in a decisive adult sense. There are a hundred reasons to excuse us from this. The most valid ones are surely the psychological complications that put people at a distance from understanding themselves.

The power to sin and the power to do good coexist in us, and they ripen as we grow. These are two aspects of the same mystery of incarnation. That is why sin is the other side of love. Our morality has the same shape as our lives. Morality, therefore, deserves to be celebrated rather than trivialized. For most people it is hard to catch anything but some glimpse of the wonder of being alive. They do see part of it now and then, but the achievement of moral maturity is arduous and sometimes beyond them. Most of us are at the beginning stages of this exploration. It is not a trip on which we throw up our hands at the world nor one that causes us to look away from or to deny our own human experience. Our morality is incarnated as we deal with the truth of ourselves, as we become ourselves in life. That we are at the early stages of this pilgrimage to maturity should not be discouraging. Indeed, one of the factors that is a great support and help to our moral awareness is the fact that we are on this journey together. We recognize our need to help each other along the way.

Morality is a sign of our individual presence, one that is, however, intertwined at every stage with the way we live with other persons. Morality is something we help each other to achieve because it is the evidence of our life style, the symbol of our concern for other persons as well as of our readiness to reach out and to care for them. That is precisely why we need morally committed institutions like Churches to provide communities in which we can view each other as persons sharing similar challenges and struggles. Churches are meant to create environments in which the mystery of incarnation can be pursued and celebrated. Indeed, everything connected with a living Church should be ordered to the support and sustenance of those trying to come to terms with the meaning of their lives. The slogan "support life" is severely limited if it is only applied in the anti-abortion crusade. In fact, this slogan cannot be seen in perspective unless the Churches provide the atmosphere in which a regard and struggle for all of life is paramount.

People need a sense that others recognize their difficulties, that people have passed through these problems before, that God himself understands and responds to the human situation. We need religious symbols to identify and to support our moral style. This is the business of organized religion. Unfortunately, it is still true that many churchmen remain at a fairly primitive level, both of religion and of moral teaching. And, although they are their guardians, they have little understanding of symbols. They try to coerce and control behavior, and they use the threats from worn-out myths in order to do this. As long as this attitude toward morality prevails, the Churches will only be puzzled at their failure to help mature the conscience of society.

It is easy to see that most persons have a deep longing to lead morally good lives. Most persons who are unobstructed by characterological difficulties or psychological deficits want to do the right thing with their lives. They are enemies neither to goodness nor to each other. They just find that it is difficult to understand how to live a moral life at the present time, and they need some common sense about how to live the good life. The problem for most good people is that they have been trained to think that the law is more important than their inner struggles for fuller personal responsibility. They have been all too well trained to expect moral guidance to come from outside of them. This dependence on the judgments of others markedly hampers them in their efforts to use themselves well in life. This is presently more difficult because the moral tradition built on such dependent relationships between moral guides and moral subjects no longer works well. The tradition became empty because it lost touch with the intrinsic meaning of morality. In the long run, the motivation and sensitivity to the self that delivers a genuine moral style depends on the ability of people to get in touch with the practical truth about themselves.

Indeed, if the outside of the person is the territory governed by the Commandments, the inside of persons is the homeland of the Beatitudes. These have to do with the dispositions of the heart, with the attitudes of the inner person, with the down-to-earth struggle that we all must conduct finally for ourselves about good and evil. To say that we must now look more deeply than ever within ourselves is not to abandon the meaning of Christianity in favor of some new psychological self-awareness. It is to discover where the center of gravity for our Christian moral life has always been. To say that we must examine our inner selves does not mean that we are to stand in isolation from each other before God. It is partial recognition of the fact that we are never wholly separate but that we are involved in the human situation with each other with an intimacy almost beyond description. We affect each other all the time, whether we want to admit it or not. The mystery of life centers on our realization of these invisible realities of our human exchange. Most of our good and evil is involved in the way we reach out and deal with each other. We are encouraged by the fact that we can reach and understand each other, that we can touch and change each other. This is what lightens the journey and makes us strong enough to look within to discover who we are. A moral journey is never something to be made alone, but something to be made in the company of those who understand and appreciate the struggles of the human situation. It is a mysterious and a mystical journey that we make together because it reveals how and when the Spirit gives us life. Nobody can write the intricacies of our inner moral lives into a few laws; the Christian pilgrimage depends on an inner sense of direction more than on signposts. What people do need is confidence in their own wishes to do the right thing with their lives. They need to be helped to understand their own power and opportunity to shape their moral destiny. If this means we are well rid of both hellfire as a deterrent and the vision of heaven held out as a reward, the price is well worth it. These extrinsic persuaders may have helped people control their behavior, but they may also have kept them from getting down to the roots of their intrinsic moral identity.

People who want to do the right thing recognize it in the sense of wholeness they have about their behavior. They actually sense that things fit together when they make hard but honest and sensitive decisions. The worst difficulty is that ordinary people are not taken seriously by so many of those who are in a position to assist them to achieve higher moral development. It hurts people when they do not feel regarded or treated as persons who have a special dignity and great possibilities of growth. The abiding sacrilege is that which is committed by superficial religionists who are unwilling to make the journey into the inner self with their people. They stand on the outside of them saying the same old things about the same old issues, displaying little awareness of how far ahead of them most of their people are.

Nothing frustrates the development of moral style more than superficial or extrinsic religion, which treats both good and evil in an immature and unappreciative manner. Perhaps the best recent example of this was found in the film *The Exorcist*, in which everything that is important about human beings was trivialized in the name of a magical-like religion that disregarded moral purpose and responsibility and reduced our passage through life to a product of chance and superstition. Adult morality's greatest adversary is calcified religion, smug in its own irrelevance, mistaking its own deadness for an eternal stability.

Purveyors of such religion cannot understand the pains and longings of ordinary persons. They have lost the common touch and, along with it, common sense. Because most people want to do the right thing with their lives, they are unhappy—although they cannot recognize the reason for it —when their religion provides neither the understanding nor the symbols through which they can grasp the meaning of their lives. People become discontent when the vehicles of meaning are rusted and abandoned by the institutions, like Churches, that are their custodians. There seems little help available for their search inside themselves. All too often, people are considered a market, the cannon fodder of commercialism, whether it is that of the entertainment industry or the religion industry. Perceiving persons as consumers whose steady contributions support industries or institutions deprives them of the opportunity to develop a

moral style. Such an approach offers people rules and slogans
even when they cry out that they want and need something
more than these. Religious leaders would be surprised to
find that good persons would respond if the leaders could
only speak in a common-sense language to them about their
struggle to lead good lives.

Most persons do not feel dangerously free. If anything,
in the century that has listened to so much rhetoric about
human freedom, people feel trapped. They do not feel that
they have as many choices as they would like, and so they
try to do the best they can in circumstances that seem to
confine their spirit and multiply their frustrations. They realize that freedom is out there somewhere, but they do not
know how to break through to it. They do not reach it
through giving up their obligations but through understanding them more fully. It is not in finding a new life style but
in finding their own lives and their own individual meanings
that they experience the redemption they long for.

The liberation theme, so prominent in discussions connected with the religion in the Third World, needs immediate and direct application to the life of people in
contemporary North America. They need to be freed from
the foreshortened and narrow moral parameters that have
kept them on the outside of life looking in. They need the
encouragement to begin the journey inward first to the discovery and then to the slow but sure experience of their
freedom. Common sense, built on common observations of
ourselves and others, tells us that most people may toy with
the idea of license at one time or another but that something
deep within them moves them toward a more satisfying understanding of freedom. That is the freedom Robert Frost
once described as being "easy in harness." It is not free of
others, or of demands, or of obligations, surely not unfet-
tered by the challenge of individual growth and personal
development. Humanity needs a moral sense based on com-

mon sense, and a theology that liberates them sufficiently to identify the central mystery of their existence. We are caught up in it, all of us, in the sweep as wide as history and as long as time, yet fresh for each of us, of incarnation. It is the central mystery of life and therefore of religion, and the way we enter it and experience it defines us as moral persons. We are saved by a sense of our common vocation to find and experience life rather than to clutch it obsessively as a treasure that might easily be lost. It is common sense to understand that the life God promises us is stronger, grander, and far less fearful than that.